MW01489509

MADEIRA

TRAVEL GUIDE

2024

Emerald Enchantment: Unveiling Nature's Mysteries and Cultural Wonders

WARDENS FEET

TABLE OF CONTENTS

INTRODUCTION TO MADEIRA

There's a single emerald among the immense wonders of nature's tapestry, a gem where the sea and the land dance in a never-ending display of beauty and mystery. It's a location where towering peaks embrace the sky, where the ocean's embrace is a dreamy blue, and where verdant forests mutter stories about the passage of time. It's Madeira, an island that calls the daring spirit to discover its enchanted mysteries and transcends the everyday.

As a lowly visitor who has had the good fortune to set foot on this paradise, I stand before you and can't help but describe in words the vivid tapestry that is Madeira. Envision a world where untamed mountains pierce the turquoise sky, where gentle waves from the sea caress the shore, and where emerald forests hide their secrets beneath a canopy of lush greenery. This is a sensory-awakening environment where every breath is an elixir of energy and every step takes you right into the heart of the magnificence of nature.

The Emerald Isle: A Canvas of Nature

Madeira, sometimes called the "Emerald Isle," is a revelation for people who wish to experience a closer relationship with nature. This Portuguese archipelago, tucked away in the Atlantic Ocean, has a terrain that is so varied as to beggar the imagination. Imagine impossibly high cliffs that resemble the edge of the earth itself, daring you to peer down into the chasm. Imagine terraced vineyards that exhibit human creativity by cascading down slopes in a show that appears to defy gravity.

Madeira's rough terrain captures the soul of the island. One of the highest peaks on the island, Pico do Arieiro, stands watch over you, daring you to aim higher. Ascending, the landscape below unfolds into a breathtaking green and sapphire tapestry that humbles and astounds you. It's a metaphor for life itself, where the view becomes more stunning as you ascend higher.

However, Madeira's charm extends beyond great heights. Its shoreline, a union of oceanic poetry and volcanic rock, is evidence of the ongoing struggle between land and water. Seawater and human spirits can find refuge at the Natural Pools of Porto Moniz, which have been shaped by the unrelenting waves. You can dive into the Atlantic here, feeling its chilly embrace as a symbol of rebirth.

Forest Whispers: An Orchestra of Green

A spot where time itself seems to slow down awaits you as you go deeper into Madeira. An example of the island's resilience is the old Laurissilva Forest, which is recognized as a UNESCO World Heritage Site. It's a location where the lush canopy overhead transforms sunlight into a shattered mosaic of emerald, bewitching everyone who steps inside.

I could not shake the feeling that I was a guest at a timeless dinner as I wandered through the meandering Levada roads that crisscross the woodland. Every step carried a whisper of long-forgotten secrets, and the air was heavy with the aroma of earth and moss. With their twisted roots and gnarled limbs, the trees themselves seem to be storytellers, sharing tales of adaptability and resiliency.

The island's irrigation system, known as the Levadas, is a metaphor for how human innovation can coexist peacefully with the natural world. Strolling alongside these tranquil streams will reveal undiscovered waterfalls, unique vegetation, and a feeling of being a part of life itself. It serves as a reminder that in Madeira, the most basic adventures can result in the most meaningful discoveries.

Gourmet Delights: A Sensational Feast

Enjoying Madeira's delectable cuisine is a must-do while visiting. Imagine sitting down to dinner in a charming village by the shore, where the abundance of the sea kisses the catch of the day as it is served to your table. The flavors represent the island's many cultural influences in a symphony of tastes. Portuguese, African, and Caribbean flavors coexist harmoniously throughout every meal.

Don't pass up the chance to try the renowned Espetada, which are delicious skewers of marinated meat or seafood that are grilled over an open flame. When you pair it with a perfectly aged Madeira wine, you'll feel as though you're tasting history. Like its inhabitants, the island's perseverance is symbolized by this wine, which is renowned for its depth and complexity.

Enter the lively Mercado dos Lavradores, where booths brimming with colorful flowers, unique fruits, and handcrafted items await you. It's a multisensory spectacular that symbolizes the rich cultural and traditional tapestry of the island. Here you can admire handcrafted baskets that embody the spirit of Madeira and savor passion fruit as delicious as a lover's kiss.

A Dynamic Culture: Celebrations and Customs

Madeira's soul is found not only in its flavors and sceneries but also in its lively culture. Imagine yourself engrossed in the exuberant revelries of a neighborhood festival, as vibrant parades, music, and dance fill the streets. It's an invitation to partake in the celebration and a metaphor for the island's boundless energy.

The melancholic melody of Madeira's traditional music, known as fado, evokes strong emotions. Its depressing overtones serve as a metaphor for the history of the island, which is characterized by fortitude in the face of hardship. You will experience a sense of connection to the center of Madeira, where the past and present converge, while you listen to the beautiful tunes.

CHAPTER 1

Welcome to Madeira

Why Visit Madeira?

Why travel to Madeira? Visiting Madeira is a once-in-a-lifetime opportunity. Amazing scenery, a lovely sea surrounding the island with whales and dolphins, mouthwatering food, and incredibly kind people await you!

Should that not be sufficient to persuade you to visit Madeira, you should be aware that the island is accessible year-round. Go to Madeira for some sunlight and mild weather if you wish to avoid the severe winters experienced by the rest of Europe!

Madeira is easily accessible from the rest of Europe with a few hours' flight. The top ten reasons to travel to Madeira are mentioned below:

Reason 1: Year-round good weather

The average annual temperature in Madeira is between 18 and 24° C. You can never be too hot or too chilly! You can experience Madeira's natural beauty year-round because of its ideal temperature. Hike Ponta de São Lourenço, bathe in the natural pool at Porto Moniz, and so much more!

One of the best excuses to travel to Madeira is this!

Reason 2: Go To Madera to See Its Gorgeous Landscapes

The volcanic archipelago of Madeira is located in the center of the Atlantic Ocean and offers a diverse and exotic environment together with a very warm temperature. Madeira, which is off the coasts of Portugal and Morocco, is endowed with stunning and varied scenery. It feels like a garden, the entire island. There are flowers all everywhere.

There are beaches with golden or black sand after that. Additionally, Ponta de São Lourenço offers a lunar-like scenery, and there are amazing mountains like Pico do Arieiro and Pico Ruivo! Additionally, you may walk atop Europe's tallest cliff! That is accurate.

Reason 3: Madeira is a reasonably priced destination

Madeira is still far less expensive when compared to other European islands like Corsica or the Canary Islands. First off, there are inexpensive flights to Madeira, such those operated by EasyJet. You can travel there for less than 50 euros per person if you make reservations in advance! Not too terrible, huh?

The majority of Madeira's tourist attractions are free because they primarily entail hiking through breathtaking scenery, relaxing on the beach, and seeing lovely natural areas.

Additionally reasonably priced and offering good value are hotels.

Reason 4: Travel to Funchal, the stunning city and Madeiran historical capital.

The capital and largest city of the island of Madeira is Funchal. There are several taverns, restaurants, and stores in its historic center. The Monte Palace Gardens, a must-see in Madeira, are among the most spectacular botanic areas on earth. You may also schedule a cable car ride from Funchal to get there.

5) Joy: Appreciate One Of The World's Most Amazing Carnivals

The carnival takes place forty days before to Easter. A customary procession and a prominent occasion in Madeira, drawing spectators from around the globe to witness the superbly orchestrated Samba groups that enliven the streets of Funchal with melodies and rhythms.

There are two carnival parades; the biggest, the Allegoric Parade (Cortejo Alegórico), featuring vibrant costumes, is held on Saturday night. The most anticipated and funniest procession is the final one on Tuesday, the Humorous procession (o Trapalhão), which is well-known for its comedy and social satire.

If you are visiting Madeira at that time, make sure not to miss this event!

Reason 6: The Food Tastes Amazing

First of all, Madeira produces incredibly delicious fruits and veggies! To experience the quality and freshness of Madeira's food, visit the market in Funchal, which is brimming with fruit, vegetables, and seafood.

When ordering food on the street, don't forget to get a Bolo de Caco, a circular Madeiran flatbread that can be stuffed with cheese or any other kind of filling. Delish.

One of the most well-known locations in Madeira, Kampo and Akua by chef Julio Pereira, are among the greatest restaurants in the area. Visit Maktub de Paul do Mar, a surfer haven where you can have mouthwatering fish dishes and caipirinha, for something more casula. Life is too good to be true!

And lastly, don't forget to sample Madeira wine! Blandy's Wine Lodge is one of the most well-known locations for doing this. For those who would like to sample something more exceptional, consider a poncha. a punch made with honey, local rhum, and fruit.

Reason 7: The Hiking Paradise Of Madeira

On the flight to Madeira, you will quickly realize that the island is a hiking enthusiast's dream come true. In fact, to save space on their luggage, the majority of people will already be wearing their hiking shoes. In Madeira, hiking shoes are a requirement! Hiking is also another essential activity!

Madeira has a ton of fantastic hiking routes. Select a handful of the more well-liked ones if you are only planning to remain for a week or a few days. For a very distinct Madeira environment, we heartily suggest visiting Ponta de São Lourenço or Levada do Caldeirão Verde. Additionally, Pico do Arieiro and Pico Ruivo offer access to the summit of Madeira.

Reason 8: Relax At One Of Portugal's Most Amazing Beaches

Go to the neighboring island of Madeira, Porto Santo, to find a 9-kilometer beach with fine golden sand and crystal clear water. We completely see why this location has been named as one of Portugal's top beaches! It's very breathtaking.

You will need to take a ferry from Madeira to Porto Santo.

Reason 9: You Can Go To The Favorite Town Of Winston Churchill

Explore Câmara de Lobos, a quaint seaside town in Madeira. The town that Winston Churchill loved. We cordially welcome you to explore Câmara de Lobos, a charming seaside community including cobblestone lanes, a beach, a seaside promenade, and colorful fishing boats.

Câmara de Lobos was one of the highlights of our Madeira vacation for us. Its proximity to Funchal further enhances its convenience of visitation.

REASON #10: Madeira has been named the world's best island destination numerous times!

Madeira Island has been named the finest island destination in Europe seven times in the last eight years, and it was chosen as the world's top destination by the World Travel Awards for the sixth consecutive year. Amazing, isn't it? Therefore, it's not just us who believe that Madeira is a fantastic destination.

You most likely have enough motivations now to travel to Madeira. Don't hesitate any longer—plan your trip to this amazing island right away!

How to Get to Madeira

Madeira may only be reached by boat or airplane.

You have a few flight alternatives if you are departing from the UK. Direct flights are available from every major airport in the United Kingdom, as well as numerous smaller airports such as Leeds, Luton, Bristol, and Newcastle. And this little island becomes quite accessible in less than 4 hours of flight time.

I strongly advise arriving in Lisbon by plane and taking a flight to the island from there if you are traveling from the US. (If Lisbon is new to you, see my First Timers Guide to Lisbon.) There are numerous daily flights available from the Portuguese mainland, so your alternatives are numerous.

Azores Airlines does, however, offer a single weekly direct flight from Madeira to JFK.

Because Madeira Airport is so little, you should avoid arriving too early for your flight.

After passing through security, follow the signs to the smoking area, which is a sizable outdoor balcony where you can sit and watch jets land in one of the most difficult airports in the world. really cool

There are many ships that spend half or full days in Madeira if you're enjoying the cruise life. The majority of cruises dock at Funchal, so schedule your day appropriately or look for a very uncommon cruise that spends more than a day in Madeira. Madeira is a stop on the majority of cruises that are branded as "Canary Islands Tours".

CHAPTER 2

Planning Your Trip
Best Time to Visit

Are you wondering what the best time of the year to visit Madeira? Well the good news, is that Madeira is an all year round destination. However, to avoid rainy days some months are better than the others...

Located in the heart of the Atlantic, the island of Madeira has a subtropical climate. Temperatures are mild all year round.

The middle of winter brings temperatures that rarely fall below 15 degrees, usually hovering around 20.

Summertime temperatures rarely rise beyond 25 degrees, so don't expect oppressive heat like in some regions of Europe.

Although it is possible to visit the island year-round, April through August is the ideal period to go in order to avoid rainy days and enjoy most of the blue skies during your trip.

You won't have to worry about lacking sunshine if you were planning to visit Madeira in other months of the year.

Let's look at it in more details in the break down below:

WHEN TO VISIT MADEIRA? WINTER TO SKIP THE CROWD AND ENJOY SOME WARMER DAYS COMPARED TO THE REST OF EUROPE!

Temperatures fluctuate on average between 15°C at night and 20°C during the day in winter in Madeira. With the rain, the weather can change rapidly.

Between October and February is when it rains the most, and it can be very windy.

Therefore, if you want to go on excursions or trek in the mountains, exercise caution and pay close attention to the weather prediction.

For our part, we spent a month in February traveling to Madeira.

We could have easily spent many days lounging on the beach, and we had fantastic days.

Even if there were a few days with a lot of rain, particularly in the north, the temperature was still substantially higher than it was in the rest of Europe.

WHEN TO GO TO MADEIRA? IN SPRING TO SEE THE ISLAND FULL OF COLOURFUL FLOWERS

Spring is certainly one of the most pleasant seasons to visit Madeira. During this period, the temperatures vary respectively from 17 to 20°C. In June, you might see a light cloud cover in the mornings, which the locals refer to as the "capacete". But this disappears as the day progresses. Between May and August, rain showers are infrequent. Indeed, the rainy season ends in April

Spring is ideal for going on a hike and discovering the stunning landscapes that the island has to offer. Remember that May is when the flower festival, the most well-known celebration in the archipelago, takes place. Everywhere on the island is covered in vibrant flowers.

WHEN TO GO TO MADEIRA? IN SUMMER FOR THE WARMEST DAYS AND BLUE SKY

Summertime temperatures range from an average of 20°C to a maximum of 25–26°C during the day.

But because Madeira draws a lot of people, summer is the busiest time to visit. Thus, if you prefer solitude when exploring Madeira's main attractions or going on a trek, consider traveling there in the spring or fall.

A TIME TO GO TO MADERA? TO ENJOY THE ISLAND BY YOURSELF IN AUTUMN

Even though there will be more rain during this season, it is still a perfect time to visit Madeira because there won't be as many tourists as there will be and the weather will still be fairly mild, with daytime highs of 24°C. The gentle water temperature makes it ideal for swimming as well.

IN MADEIRA, IS IT WINDY?

Yes, is the instant response. In Madeira, the wind might pick up a lot. Strong winds do, in fact, frequently cause flight cancellations. It is true that the aircraft are unable to touch down at the Madeira airport. That's precisely what took place with us. The wind was so bad on the day we were due to go that no plane could land or take off for two days!

Since we had plenty of time ahead of us and were on a sabbatical anyhow, we didn't really mind. We were fortunate enough to depart two days later.

During the summer, the northeast breeze is the most common in Madeira. Rainfall is brought to the island by the Azores anticyclone, which is more of a westerly wind that blows from October to March.

Generally, the island's north experiences higher winds. The clouds and gusts are blocked by the mountains that peak at an elevation of more than 1400 meters. As a result, they shield the south from wind, humidity, and rain.

WHAT IS THE MADERA WATER TEMPERATURE?

Throughout the year, the ocean's temperature varies between 18 and 23°C. The months from December through April are the coldest. So long as it's not too cold, you can swim in Madeira year-round.

Go to Porto Santo, the neighboring island, for a fantastic 7 kilometre beach if you want to enjoy some beach time while in Madeira!

DO YOU KNOW OF ANY FESTIVALS IN MADERA?

Madeira has numerous celebrations all year long. Below is a list of the key ones:

JANUARY EVENING! ONE OF THE WORLD'S BIGGEST FIREWORKS!

On January 1st, in Madeira? The place you want to be is Funchal! The amazing fireworks are regarded as some of the most impressive globally and have been inducted into the Guinness Book of World Records. As the New Year falls during Madeira's busiest season, preparations must be made well in advance. The harbor is full of cruise ships.

One of the main events in Madeira is the carnival.

The carnival takes place forty days before to Easter. A customary procession and a prominent occasion in Madeira, drawing spectators from around the globe to witness the superbly orchestrated Samba groups that enliven the streets of Funchal with melodies and rhythms. There are two carnival parades; the biggest, the Allegoric Parade (Cortejo Alegórico), featuring vibrant costumes, is held on Saturday night. The most anticipated and funniest procession is the final one on Tuesday, the Humorous procession (o Trapalhão), which is well-known for its comedy and social satire.

MADEIRA'S FLOWER FESTIVAL: A MUST SEE!

One of Madeira's most vibrant annual traditions is the Flower Festival, which takes place in the spring. Around Funchal, there are a lot of events and celebrations, such as flower-filled sidewalks, outdoor concerts, and open-air folk group dances. There are numerous floral shows as well. In their exquisitely embroidered, multicolored Madeiran costumes, numerous distinct groups form a line and dance through the streets of Funchal during the major parade. Floats are adorned with an array of Madeiran flowers.

A RECAP OF WHEN IS THE BEST TIME TO GO TO MADEIRA

Madeira is a year-round travel destination with very minor seasonal temperature variations. In any season, there are plenty of activities to do in Madeira. Those who love surfing can practice year-round and take advantage of excellent waves. Hikers may explore Madeira's many routes and witness its beautiful waterfalls. You can also go swimming any month of the year if you so choose.

Nonetheless, go to Madeira in the summer to escape wet days. Go to Madeira in the spring or fall if you want to avoid the crowds and still have ideal weather.

Length of Stay

At the absolute least, five days!

Madeira is dense, although it's not very large. Although it would seem possible to see the entire main island in a single day, I would strongly advise spending at least five days because there are so many interesting locations to see and things to try.

Although you could easily make a weekend out of a visit to the archipelago's capital, Funchal, there are so many interesting sights to take in that it would be a sin not to take advantage of them.

A mere five days will do to thoroughly enjoy Funchal, Porto Moniz, and several of the major island's natural beauties (I suggest Santana and the Levada of Caldeirão Verde as must-sees).

To see the other islands in the archipelago, at least as comfortably as one would like, five days is not enough.

Ten days is preferable.

An optimum length of stay in Madeira is ten days, which will give you plenty of time to visit the islands of Porto Santo, Desertas, and Selvagens in addition to getting to know Funchal and some of the surrounding attractions. Ten days is all you need to thoroughly explore the local offerings, provided you stay busy.

Starting in Funchal, you should travel to Porto Moniz, finish the Levada of Caldeirão Verde, visit Fanal and Cape Girão (two amazing places to see in a single day), spend a few days on the beach-ready island of Porto Santo, explore the deserted Desertas and Selvagens, visit the iconic Santana houses, and end your trip in the quaint town of Caniçal.

If you have an endless amount of vacation time, two weeks is ideal.

I would suggest staying for around two weeks if you want a more laid-back vacation with lots of time to rest and some slow days at the beach. Although the suggested plan for this trip is comparable to the one mentioned in the previous paragraph, the actual experience would be significantly different.

Being "lazy" and unhurried comes naturally in Madeira; in just two weeks, you can explore all the must-see sights without feeling rushed and fully immerse yourself in everything the archipelago has to offer.

Where to Stay

The choice of accommodations for your stay in Madeira will be influenced by your intended duration of stay as well as your travel objectives. If your visit in Madeira will be shorter than four days, I would recommend spending all of your time in the capital city of Funchal, which is the hub of activity, has a great location, and is also the focus of life there.

To see and do as much as possible without having to drive back and forth to Funchal, it makes more sense to select a few bases if you plan to remain here for five days or more.

I would suggest breaking up your journey as follows:

3–7 days in Funchal: Considering that Funchal is the largest and most convenient location on the island, it makes sense to begin and end your trip there. Between all the day trips and the city's abundance of eateries, bars, and tourist attractions, there's plenty to keep you occupied.

Two days in Santana: If hiking is your thing, you may continue on from Funchal to Santana for a few days of outdoor activities in a peaceful, secluded area.

Two days in Porto Santo: There's no better way to cap off your journey than spending a few days relaxing on the stunning white sand beaches of Porto Santo.

I would plan to spend my week or ten days in Madeira!

A little additional details about each of these suggested bases are provided below:

Funchal

The capital and largest city of the archipelago, Funchal, is by far the most obvious and practical place to base yourself while visiting Madeira. If you're traveling by automobile, you can reach almost anything on the main island in less than an hour using Funchal as your base.

One of the best places to arrange a tour to the deserted islands of Desertas and Selvagens is from Funchal.

One major benefit of establishing oneself in Funchal is having easy access to services, dining options, nightlife, and tourist attractions. Compared to Lisbon or Porto, Funchal is by no means a large city, but it offers all the amenities both residents and tourists might want.

Anywhere along the bustling Sá Carneiro Avenue, which is a popular tourist destination with a view of the ocean and the greatest area on the island for an early morning jog (believe me, I've done it) is where I suggest staying.

The city's architecture is a blend of quaint colonial-style homes, some of which are from the fifteenth century, and contemporary structures.

Santo Porto

Porto Santo has the kind of white-sand beaches that the Portuguese, and pretty much everyone else, adore, but Funchal's beaches are sometimes lackluster. Porto Santo is the ideal destination if you want to spend a few days by the sea.

Porto Santo is rather unremarkable and extremely arid, nearly desertic, in comparison to the main island. It's a great spot to unwind and spend the entire day lounging on the beach, dining at some excellent local eateries, and enjoying a few drinks at some local pubs.

The good news is that the hotels and resorts on the island are significantly less expensive than those on the main island, which is to be expected given their abundance. For 80€ or less, you can easily stay a night at a beautiful resort by the beach with a swimming pool.

Santana

For an adventure focused largely on hiking, reserve lodging in Santana. Santana is a charming little town. Santana still has a higher proportion of residents than visitors, in contrast to Funchal and Porto Santo, but it does have a lot of excellent hotels.

Santana offers two different kinds of hotels: opulent spa experiences nestled alongside the natural environment, and rustic lodgings in repurposed farm buildings. Apart from a few cultural events, Santana offers plenty of natural beauty, especially for hikers who want to tackle the must-try Levada of Caldeirão Verde and for those who enjoy sightseeing (the Fortress of Faial provides an incredible perspective of the ocean).

Currency and Budgeting

Setting up money for a 2023 vacation to Madeira

The cost of your vacation to Madeira will vary based on your spending limit and type of travel. On the other hand, the following is a generic budget planning guide:

Lodging: The price of a room can vary from about €50 per night for a cheap hostel to €200 or more for a high-end establishment. A mid-range hotel typically costs about €100 per night.

Food and drink: Dining out, particularly in tourist regions, may be somewhat costly in Madeira. But there are also lots of reasonably priced cafes and eateries. Making your own meals might help you save money as well. A mid-range restaurant's lunch costs about €20 per person on average.

Activities: Hiking, motorcycling, seeing museums, and visiting historical sites are just a few of the many things to do in Madeira. While some activities are paid for, others are free. Activities typically run about €10 per person.

Transportation: Driving is the most convenient way to move throughout Madeira. A car can be rented for about €50 per day. There is, though, a reasonably priced public transportation system as well. A bus ticket typically costs €2 for each person.

Total cost: About €1,500 would be the average cost for a seven-day trip to Madeira for two persons. This covers lodging, meals, entertainment, and travel. However, based on your vacation preferences and financial constraints, you can spend more or less.

Money

The euro (€) is the currency in use in Madeira. In banks, exchange offices, and hotels, you can exchange your local currency for euros. To obtain the greatest exchange rate, it is normally recommended to exchange your money before leaving your native country.

.

CHAPTER 3

Options for Accommodation

While there are lodging options such as hotels and Airbnbs all around Madeira, you may want to base yourself in a location that's convenient for buses and tours.

I suggest staying in Funchal if this is your first time visiting Madeira and you want to take the time to truly see the island. All year round, and throughout the day, the city center offers an abundance of buses, taxis, and tours.

In comparison to many sites in Western Europe, accommodations are incredibly affordable, with luxurious accommodations readily available for less than €200 per night!

Everything you look there are breathtaking views of the surrounding mountains and water, and you are close enough to the center to be able to walk everything. The staff is warm and helpful, the breakfast buffet is insanely large, and every room has a balcony. What more is there to ask for?

Santa Cruz is the ideal location if you like to stay nearer the airport. Additionally, the region is particularly family-friendly.

Stay at Porto Moniz if you want to be close to activities without being in a large metropolis. Nothing compares to enjoying your morning coffee while watching the waves smash against the rocks at the tidal pools, which are kind of big deal. You would be better off renting a car because Porto

Moniz is located on the exact other side of the island from the airport.

One Of The Best Areas To Stay In Madera Is Funchal.

Funchal is a beautiful city with lots to see. It's among the greatest places to stay in Madeira.

Located in the middle of Funchal are the historic Jesuit college, a lavish 16th-century cathedral, and the old city center with its many historical landmarks. You may also explore the old episcopal palace, which is now home to an art museum with a collection of Flemish paintings.

After that, you may take the cable car from Funchal to the botanical garden at Monte Palace Tropical Garden, where you can take in the breath-taking panoramic views of the city and the ocean.

These are our top picks for lodging in Funchal:

The boutique hotel Castanheiro

This gorgeous four-star hotel has an outdoor pool on its roof with views of the city. You may explore Funchal to the fullest by walking from the hotel to the ancient town! The breakfast is amazing, the accommodations are extremely pleasant, and the service is excellent! One of our top picks for lodging in Funchal is this one.

Porto Santa Maria Hotel

This little hotel in Funchal is well situated near the harbor and offers all you need for the ideal Madeira vacation! There are expansive views of the Atlantic from this hotel. It includes restaurants, a spa, and two pools. We adore Santa Maria's location since it offers a breathtaking view of the sea while being right in the middle of Funchal.

Living in Funchal X

Choose Living Funchal X if your trip to Madeira is more tightly budgeted. This recently refurbished apartment is in the ideal location in Funchal's old town. Numerous eateries, pubs, supermarkets, and other stores are located nearby! We stayed there for several nights and were not let down.

Câmara de Lobos

This small fishing village, which is west of Funchal, has remained true to itself over time. One of our favorite meals in Madeira is scabbardfish, which is one of the best seafood dishes to try at this charming little fishing harbor with its vibrant boats!

Aside from its rich historical background, Câmara de Lobos is home to two of Madeira's most important sites: the chapel of Nossa Senhora da Conceição and the church of São Sebastião.

Câmara de Lobos is one of the greatest places to stay in Madeira because of its close vicinity to Cabo Girao, the highest cliff in Europe with a breathtaking vista on a glass platform, and other major attractions.

Where can I stay in Câmara de Lobos? These hotels are our top picks.

Pestana Churchill Bay

Pestana Churchill Bay, one of our favorite hotels in Madeira, is situated near Câmara de Lobos. This former fish market was converted into a stunning hotel close to the harbor. The hotel is gorgeous, in the ideal location, and has a rooftop pool with breathtaking views of Câmara de Lobos.

Pestana Fishermen Village

Pestana Fisherman Village in Câmara de Lobos is another amazing boutique hotel. The charming historic center is where this hotel is situated.

The hotel has many living areas, a cloister, a library, a patio with a water mirror, and a rooftop terrace with a panoramic pool.

The best place to stay in the northern Madeira region is Porto Moniz.

This city, which is northwest of Madeira, is well-known for its stunning natural pools that were created by volcanic lava. If you want to unwind and take in the stunning views of the island's natural formations, this is the ideal spot to stay in Madeira.

Porto Moniz also has a wide variety of cafes and an endless supply of seafood eateries.

Seixal, Santana, Fanal Forest, Miradouro do Véu da Noiva, and many other places are conveniently accessible from there.

One of the best treks on the island is the Levada da Ribeira da Janela, which will enchant hikers no matter how hard they try. You will be able to explore a variety of vistas along this path, which alternates between verdant valleys and towering mountains.

As such, one of the greatest places to stay in Madeira is Porto Moniz.

Our list of the top hotels in Porto Moniz is as follows:

Pearls Beach apartment

The Pearls Beach Apartment in the heart of Porto Moniz offers opulence along with a breathtaking view of the sea. The nature pools are just a short stroll from this ideal location! The living room, kitchen, and patio area are all separate from the apartment.

Pearls Beach Villa

This gorgeous property in the heart of Porto Moniz is highly recommended if you're looking for the utmost in comfort and luxury during your time in Madeira. The villa has three bedrooms, two of which have en suite bathrooms, a living room, a TV room, a BBQ, and additional areas for relaxation. Don't hesitate to visit this location if you are a large family or group.

Casa de Levada, our all-time favorite hotel!

We have never stayed in a more delightful place than Casa de Levada. The room is exquisite, with a breathtaking view of the ocean and Madeira. The room's small elements are all very well thought out. The hobbit bar was a hit, and the pool is gorgeous. What a wonderful location to stay. I can't suggest staying here to anyone enough.

CHAPTER 4

How to Navigate Madeira

It is more difficult, but not impossible, to go around without a car in the absence of a train system.

You can simply choose from a plethora of tour packages available on Viator and Get Your Guide to see the island's top attractions in two or three days. An open top 4x4 private tour is the greatest way to see the island and experience Madeira authentically, and I can't recommend it enough.

If you're not a big fan of excursions, you can travel the entire island by bus. You may even get a day ticket and jump on and off whenever and anywhere you like. Tickets are quite inexpensive.

You can rent a car if you're feeling really daring, but be warned—some of the roads are not for the timid. Avoid driving in Madeira if you're afraid of heights, as some of the roads barely hang on to the edge of sheer cliffs without any safety barriers.

The V1, the island's single freeway, circles the entire island. If you're feeling peckish, you can schedule your day travels to destinations off the V1.

Everyone can get a taxi, and they can even arrange for day trips throughout the island for you. This is the ideal choice if you wish to spend some time at a particular location rather than traveling back and forth. Although they cost a little more than using Viator to plan a tour, at least you can come and go as often as you'd like.

Across the island of Madeira, there are seven cable car systems that are ideal for traveling from the base to the summit of the mountain and back. You won't have to trek all the way to the summit if you take a bus or taxi to the cable car station, of course.

CHAPTER 5

Top Travel Destinations: Funchal

If you want to have a good time, check out a variety of interesting restaurants, and mingle with the people, Funchal is the place to be in Madeira.

Funchal, the sixth-most populous city in Portugal, is located in a natural valley on the southwest coast of the main island of Madeira. Modern structures, exquisitely restored homes in the colonial style, and quaint old fishermen's houses—some of which have been turned into pubs and restaurants—combine to form the city's architecture.

The old part of Funchal is centered on Santa Maria Street, which is lined with interesting street art.

The population of Funchal is highly diversified. The city is visited by Portuguese natives, an increasing number of young expats, and a small but diversified population of college students (attending the local University of Madeira). At times, the area feels highly touristy, and visitors do abound.

Eating lunch at Mozart and then taking a thrilling ride on the Funchal-Monte cable car (which stops directly in front of the restaurant) is one of my favorite afternoon activities in the city.

I suggest going for a swim at Barreirinha Beach, one of the city's liveliest night destinations, if the weather permits (which it always does).

There's a pretty fun jam at Café Museu most Thursday nights. It's a great chance to meet the hippest, most culture-conscious folks in Funchal and is being hosted by some of my closest friends on the island.

Santo Porto

For beachheads visiting Madeira, the island of Porto Santo—which is reachable by ferry—must be visited. With so many rocks and a turbulent surf, the beaches on the main island can be a little uncomfortable; nevertheless, Porto Santo is essentially a large white-sand beach.

Personally, I think Zimbralinho Beach and Fontinha Beach are the two most beautiful beaches in Porto Santo. Additionally, they are very different; the latter is great for families, while the former is less accessible yet great for diving and other outdoor/water sports.

Why are my favorite beaches at Porto Santo, Zimbralinho and Fontinha? Zimbralinho, the island's most naturally stunning beach, is difficult to get to despite having steep cliffs that overlook the sea. Not only is Zimbralinho a great place for photos, but it's also well-known for its very swimmable natural ponds that emerge in some of the rocks during low tide.

I adore Fontinha because it's a traditional, family-friendly, easily accessible white sand beach that's ideal for senior travelers, families with little children, and anybody else wanting to unwind by the seaside.

Desertas and Selvagens

The two other islands in the Madeira archipelago are minuscule in size, consisting of tiny islands formed by rocks. It's little wonder they're dubbed Selvagens and Desertas (which translate as "Savages" and "Deserted"), as there are plenty of natural resources and no one lives there.

If you want to spend a pleasant day at the beach with friends and family, be sure to check out Selvagens and Desertas, which are accessible by boat from the mainland.

In addition to offering visitors the opportunity to walk about some of the islands, boat tours to the Selvagens and Desertas typically concentrate on the marine life that surrounds the small archipelagos—whale and dolphin sightings are common.

Cancio

Caniçal, a must-see location in Madeira, is thirty minutes' drive from Funchal. Caniçal, a civil parish of the municipality of Machico, is located near the westernmost point of the main island of Madeira. Though it is a small town with fewer than 4,000 inhabitants, Caniçal is a popular tourist destination because to its amazing oceanside islets and local cuisine.

The primary sites are situated adjacent to each other. There is the beach called Praínha (roughly, "small beach"), which is encircled by rocks, and there is the Ponta de São Lourenço, a massive cliff with an amazing perspective of the ocean.

When you grow tired of the view, Caniçal's numerous excellent (and reasonably priced) eateries are a great option. When it comes to Caniçal, Muralhas and Aquarium are my two favorite places to eat authentic Madeira cuisine.

Ocean lovers could also take advantage of the various diving and snorkeling opportunities in the town, which include the once-in-a-lifetime chance to swim alongside whales and dolphins.

Caldeirão Verde (Levada)

A specific kind of irrigation channel that is indigenous to Madeira is called a levada. The Levadas were formerly used to carry water to isolated parts of the island, but today many residents and visitors explore them for trekking.

Like ordinary walks, levadas follow winding pathways alongside the previously stated historic irrigation systems. There are plenty of Levada experiences to choose from, but the one in Caldeirão Verde is arguably the best because it passes through a lush forest and isn't too strenuous physically.

Beginning from Queimadas Forest Park, the hike concludes at Caldeirão do Inferno. While waiting, you get to view some truly breathtaking waterfalls and even a few of the classic Santana area triangle homes.

Despite being regarded as one of Madeira's easier levadas, Caldeirão Verde nevertheless takes about six and a half hours to finish.

Porto Moniz

Funchal is around an hour's drive away from Porto Moniz, a quaint Madeira town with plenty to see and do. The finest place to swim on the main island is probably Porto Moniz's natural pools, which I visit every time I visit. A €3 admission fee applies, but it's well worth it.

The water in these naturally occurring pools is always clean and fresh because waves from the ocean regularly feed them, even though they were refurbished to make them safer.

You won't be surprised if you see a lot of visitors swimming in there because the accompanying infrastructure (which includes restrooms, showers, and food services) is also really great (don't worry, though, it never gets unbearably busy).

Along with its many neighborhood eateries and cafés, Porto Moniz is well-known for its Aquarium, a modest but fascinating oceanarium. Typically, a ticket costs about 8 euros. Porto Moniz has little to see outside of the seaside area, which is home to the oceanarium and natural pools.

Santana

On the main island of Madeira, Santana is a fascinating municipality that is most recognized for its distinctive Madeirense homes. These are one of the most popular tourist destinations in Madeira and comprise an oddly shaped triangle with a distinctive thatched roof.

It would be almost criminal to visit Madeira and miss the opportunity to see Santana's homes, but there are many additional attractions in Santana. The Madeira Theme Park, which prominently displays Madeira's tradition, history, and distinctive culture, is a good illustration of such.

The Madeira Theme Park is by no means your typical theme park with rollercoasters, despite its name! The garden serves as a living outdoor museum that highlights the finest aspects of Madeira culture, such as the previously mentioned Santana houses, local food shops, traditional crafts, a playground for kids, a small farm with sheep, and a lake.

Curral das Freiras

Known as "Nun's Corral," Curral das Freiras is a tiny, incredibly remote settlement nestled in a valley amidst the mountains of Câmara de Lobos municipality.

Notwithstanding the name, the community was first established in the fifteenth century by runaway slaves who erected shacks in this remote location instead of nuns.

These days, Curral das Freiras is a lesser-known Madeira destination that should appeal especially to adventure seekers. Even with a car, getting there is somewhat difficult, but the effort is worthwhile.

I feel like I've traveled to a different realm each time I enter Curral das Freiras.

São Vicente Caves

The São Vicente Caves are a geological marvel that you must see if you're anywhere near São Vicente and you like cavern exploration. These are the only volcanic caves in all of Portugal that are open to the public, and they were formed almost a million years ago.

They're temporarily closed as I write this, but don't hesitate to visit when they're open to the public again!

Cascata dos Anjos

The area around Ponta do Sol is home to not just my favorite hotel in Madeira, the stunning and contemporary Estalagem da Ponta do Sol, but also one of the island's best-kept secrets, the Cascata dos Anjos, or "Angels's Waterfall".

Best feature? The waterfall pours over a section of the former E.R. 101 regional road, making it accessible by car. The entire journey is worth taking, but exercise caution—it only takes one false turn to end up in the ocean!

Cape Girão

Cape Girão, the highest cliff skywalk in Europe, is another must-see natural feature in Madeira. For those who are terrified of heights, Cape Girão can be frightening, but it also offers one of the most breathtaking views you'll ever see.

Girão is the must-see cliff in Madeira where the full force of the island's natural beauty is most evident.

Hike from Pico do Areeiro to Pico Ruivo

The trail leading from Pico do Areeiro to Pico Ruivo, Madeira's highest point, can be rather strenuous, in contrast to the comparatively easy Levada of Caldeirão Verde climb. However, it's the kind of Madeira experience you shouldn't pass up if you like challenging yourself and you think your physical health is good.

If you have the necessary legs, you may finish the 11-kilometer (about 6.8-mile) hike in less than four hours. However, it's not only a "athletic" experience. The hike from Pico do Areeiro to Pico Ruivo is incredibly beautiful and challenging. I wholeheartedly urge you to pursue photography if you enjoy it.

Fanal

I vividly recall my first visit to Fanal, a sizable forested area close to the Seixal region. Fanal is ideal for summer strolls, but it's also easily reachable by automobile (the route is actually pretty lovely). Wintertime fanal can also be quite lovely, provided you remember to bring along a good jacket.

There are times when the wind is so intense that it feels like it will knock you down!

Fanal is, nevertheless, a kind of Madeira's Shire (yeah, there was a Lord of the Rings reference!) and a spot where one can feel completely inspired when the weather is right. Fanal is sometimes called "mystical," and I wholeheartedly concur.

The main island has many beautiful natural places, but there's something special about Fanal that makes me want to return.

Paul da Serra

Having previously experienced Fanal's natural attractions, how about making a short diversion to take a scenic drive through the Paul da Serra highlands? The Paul da Serra road is, for me, the best in all of Madeira; it's a desolate area populated mostly by roaming cattle and massive wind turbines (for a vehicle ride, not for hiking).

CR7 Museum

To be completely honest, I wouldn't advise every traveler to Madeira to visit the CR7 Museum in Funchal. However, the museum is worth seeing if one of the factors that led you to decide to visit the archipelago as your next vacation spot is Cristiano Ronaldo.

One of the most well-known sports stars in the world, Cristiano Ronaldo is also one of Madeira's most recognizable cultural icons—yes, I'm talking about the Santana homes, the poncha, and the Levada treks!

Whether we like it or not, learning about Ronaldo's past is similar to learning about Madeira's past. Ronaldo is the most significant historical figure, the indisputable folk hero, and the prodigal son of Madeira—even if he is still alive.

CHAPTER 6

Outdoor Actitvities

1. GET STARTED WITH FUNCHAL, MADEIRA'S BEAUTIFUL CAPITAL!

With 110,000 residents, this charming town serves as both Madeira's capital and largest metropolis. It has a wealth of interesting areas of interest and serves as the island's political, cultural, and economic center. Of course, Funchal should be the first site you visit when looking for things to do in Madeira.

It is definitely worthwhile to explore the historical center and its harbor. We suggest visiting Santa Maria's Mercado dos Lavradores, a vibrant farmers' market with adorned doors.

Take a minimum of one or two days to explore Funchal.

2. GO TO THE MOST BEAUTIFUL GARDEN IN MADEIRA, MONTE PALACE MADEIRA!

Do you remain in Funchal? Exactly! See Monte Palace Madeira, one of the most magnificent gardens we have ever seen, perched atop the city! To get to this amazing garden, ride the well-known cable car in Funchal's downtown.

It is a definite must to visit Monte Palace Madeira when visiting Madeira.

There are two things you can do after the park visit. Take the second cable car to Madeira Botanical Garden to continue your trip.

The alternative choice is to descend using a well-known, diminutive wicker sled that is representative of Funchal! These are classic tuk-tuks from Madagascar! Their wooden runners, driven by two experienced pilots, will provide you with the excitement of returning to Funchal's old core.

3. GARDEN MADEIRA BOTANICAL

There is a second cable car right adjacent to Monte Palace Garden that makes it simple to get to this second garden. A collection of more than 2,000 plants from all over the world can be admired there. Beautiful collections of palm trees, several orchid species, cacti, and much more may be found.

There are breathtaking views of Funchal and its surrounds from the garden that looks out over the city.

It will take at least three to five hours to see both gardens. It will take some time to ride the cable car because both gardens are very large. The simplest route back to Funchal is to descend the Cable Car.

Although there isn't much to see on the way down, the streets are rather steep and it is possible to stroll back to Funchal. In Funchal, you can buy a round-trip cable car ticket that includes admission to both parks.

4. GO ON A BOAT TRIP TO VIEW WHALES AND DOLPHINS

It's time to take a boat tour of the stunning island of Madeira after taking in the breathtaking view of the island from the Gardens.

Not only will you get to see Madeira from a different perspective, but if you're lucky, you might even get to see whales and dolphins. You can even jump in the water in the summer.

Our boat excursion was scheduled through Magic Dolphins. Dolphins were everywhere we saw during our trip, playing. On our first day in Madeira, this happened!

We are off to the best start to our vacation ever.

5. See Câmara de Lobos, Winston Churchill's favorite town.

Explore Câmara de Lobos, a quaint seaside town in Madeira. The town that Winston Churchill loved. We cordially welcome you to explore Câmara de Lobos, a charming seaside community including cobblestone lanes, a beach, a seaside promenade, and colorful fishing boats, among many other attractions.

Câmara de Lobos was one of the highlights of our Madeira vacation for us. It is also rather convenient to visit because it is close to Funchal.

Because to Câmara de Lobos' appeal, it is one of Madeira's most popular tourist destinations. The black basalt rock, which contrasts with the turquoise seas, formed a lengthy natural harbor around which the building was constructed. It's a stunning and incredibly gorgeous location.

In 1950, Winston Churchill, the former prime minister of Great Britain, traveled to Madeira. He remained in Câmara de Lobos throughout his journey, where he created a superb image of the community. Câmara de Lobos is still remembered for his visit today, and numerous locations bear his name. There is even a statue of him in a street that faces the ocean.

6. Among the world's highest cliffs is Cape Giròo.

Proceed with your tour to Cape Girão, which is around 580 meters high and is among the world's highest cliffs, after seeing Câmara de Lobos. The cliff's edge outlook is breathtaking, providing a breathtaking perspective of Câmara de Lobos, the ocean, and the Fajã do Cabo Girão.

Aside from the amazing scenery, you should be aware that base jumping and paragliding are popular activities there.

You can push yourself to the utmost on the 2012-constructed Skywalk, a hanging glass platform, especially if you're afraid of heights.

7. Ponta do Sol

You can continue exploring the southern region of Madeira in Ponta do Sol after visiting Cape Girão. During your trip to Madeira, you should definitely visit this lovely village by the sea!

See the inside of the Church of Nossa Senhora da Luz, stroll through the vibrant seaside alleys, and take in the stunning Palacete do Lugar de Baixo, also known as Palacete dos Zinos, which was converted into a boutique hotel in the beginning of 2020.

8. Drive through the most distinctive waterfall in Madeira, Anjos Waterfall!

One of our favorites, Anjo's Waterfall, comes next on our list. Madeira's first waterfall for you! On the island, there will be a lot more to see.

After leaving Ponta do Sol, proceed along the former route (ER101) that connects the two towns to Madalena do Mar. You will pass beneath the Dos Anjos waterfall and come across the ancient tunnels that resemble cave entrances.

Though not the most spectacular waterfall in Madeira, Anjos is unquestionably the most distinctive. A tiny road is where the waterfall finishes. Because cars are forced to pass through it, the locals refer to it as the "free car wash".

Social media helped it become well-known in recent years! We also really enjoyed it. Seeing the automobiles pass through the waterfall was entertaining.

9. Among Madeiran's best beaches is PRAIA DA CALHETA.

In Madeira, there aren't many sandy beaches. But Praia da Calheta is among the best. After Anjos Waterfall, just keep going on the coastal road, and you'll be to Praia da Calheta in 12 minutes.

On the island of Madeira, one of the most exquisite sandy beaches is Praia da Calheta. Its soft sands and convenient access make it a popular choice for both tourists and locals, despite not being as magnificent as some of the island's more picturesque beaches.

10. CURRAL DA EIRA DO SERRADO & MIRADOURO DAS FREIRAS

It's time to head further inland after touring the island's south. Begin your visitation in Curral das Freiras.

Located at the base of many mountains, Curral das Freiras is a little community that remained isolated until 1959, when the first road connecting it to the rest of the island was constructed.

The views of the mountains in the area are really stunning!

When you get there, be sure to sample the ginja (cherry liqueur) and chestnut soup, which are local specialties.

Curral das Freiras can also be appreciated from the spectacular Eira do Serrado viewpoint, which provides a panoramic perspective of this singular location and the six surrounding mountains.

11. PICO DO ARIEIRO

Pico do Arieiro, the island of Madeira's third-highest peak (1818 m), comes next on the list of must-see attractions. The view from the summit of the mountains is breathtaking!

Road access is available to Pico do Arieiro. Therefore, visiting Pico do Arieiro is a simple way to take in Madeira's breathtaking scenery if hiking isn't your thing.

Those with more sense of adventure may opt to trek rather than drive to the summit of Pico do Arieiro. Not only is this hike one of the most breathtaking, but it's also one of the riskiest. A narrow rocky trail links Pico do Arieiro with Pico Ruivo over a 7-kilometer trek.

Pack warm clothing! Temperatures at the summit can occasionally approach freezing (particularly in the winter).

12. A TRACK TO THE HIGHEST PEAK IN MADERA, PICO RUIVO

At 1,862 meters, Pico Ruivo is the highest point in Madeira and the third highest peak in Portugal, behind Torre (Serra da Estrela) and Ponta do Pico (Azores).

You will need to hike in order to get there. The route from Achada do Teixeira to Pico Ruivo (2.8 km) is the one we advise you to take. You'll love its beauty, peace, and the fact that it's atop the clouds, not to mention that it's one of the summits that's easiest to reach!

All levels of fitness can complete this trip; however, the 300 meters of elevation gain between the starting point (Achada do Teixeira) and Pico Ruivo will need an average of one and a half hours of climbing.

13. THE NATURE PARK OF RIBEIRO FRIO

It is among the greatest locations to view the breathtaking Laurissilva forest, which makes up a significant portion of the interior of the island of Madeira and is recognized by UNESCO. This area is good for nature lovers and is great for family exploration because it is home to various endemic species of both flora and animals.

Climb up to the Balcões viewpoint for a breathtaking perspective of Madeira.

You can schedule a guided tour to explore this region of Madeira without renting a car.

14. A MADEIRA MUST HAVE IS MIRADOURO DOS BALCÕES!

Situated in the Parque do Ribeiro Frio, 10 km away from Pico do Areeiro, is the magnificent Balcões viewpoint. You will have to travel the short Vereda dos Balcões walking route, which follows the Serra do Faial Levada, to reach there.

On clear days, you can view Penha d'Águia, Pico do Areeiro, and Pico Ruivo, which make up the island's center mountain range.

The numerous birdsong along the trail is another well-known feature of this trek. The birds will come and eat your snack if you hold out your palm at the lookout and place a few grains or pieces in it.

In Madeira, don't forget to pack appropriate hiking shoes. There may be mud and slippage on the ground.

15. Machico: A Delightful Spot in Madeira

Explore the eastern part of the island by starting at Machico.

About twenty-five kilometers from Funchal, the village of Machico is reputed to have been the initial landing spot when the Portuguese explorers João Gonçalves Zarco and Tristão Vaz Teixeira discovered the island at the start of the fifteenth century.

This town is situated near to two stunning beaches and has grown up along a valley.

Admire the Aqueduct of Machico, the Igreja Matriz de Machico, and the Fort of São João Baptista in addition to the natural wonders.

Make the most of your trip by hiking the Levada do Caniçal, which will provide you stunning views of Machico, the coast, and the surrounding countryside.

Levada

Levadas are found all across the island of Madeira. Some span 2,150 kilometers in total and blend in with the surrounding environment. An irrigation conduit called a levada is used to irrigate different types of agricultural land. From the sixteenth century until the 1940s, they were excavated. In Madeira, levadas are also utilized to generate electricity.

They frequently have trails around them that let visitors hike and take in the island's breathtaking scenery. When visiting Madeira, be sure to trek at least one of the Levada. Later in this piece, we'll let you know which one we think is best.

16. FAVORITE HIDING PONTA DE SÃO LOURENÇO IN MADEIRA!

Ponta de São Lourenço, one of the most striking sites in Madeira, is the next item on the list.

The appearance of São Lourenço differs greatly from the rest of Madeira. There won't be a waterfall, levada, or woodland here. It's a long, untamed peninsula with a largely arid terrain. It is still just as gorgeous as the rest of the island, though. This is indeed one of our favorite spots in Madeira!

Like Madeira's easternmost point, this location is most well-known for visits during sunrise. There's a breathtaking 7.4 kilometer hike (round trip). A tiny cafe and restaurant can be found at the tip of the Peninsula, resembling a mirage in the middle of nothing. It appears to be a desert oasis virtually. What a location!

You may even schedule a boat excursion from the restaurant to return to Madeira if you don't feel like hiking back. Details here.

When in Madeira, a trip to Ponta de São Lourenço is a must!

17. Unmissable sights to see in Madeira, Santana!

Start your visit with Santana north of Madeira.

While the village of Santana has many lovely sites to see, the most iconic aspect of the town is definitely its distinctive thatched-roof dwellings. These days, the houses serve as neighborhood stores. Make sure to include this on your schedule as it is a must-see attraction in Madeira.

Due to the abundance of natural resources in the area, including the Laurissilva Forest, home to numerous indigenous species of local flora and fauna, the entire municipality of Santana has been designated by UNESCO as a Biosphere Reserve. islands. The highest peaks in Madeira, Pico Ruivo, Pico das Torres, and Pico do Areeiro, are also located here.

18. MIRADOURO DA BEIRA DA QUINTA

You must be familiar with a few terms in Madeira. One is Levada, which we have already discussed in this piece. You'll also hear the word "miradouro" a lot. You will come across numerous road signs reading "Miradadouro" when traveling through Madeira. Those are perspectives!

A well-known one in Madeira is called Miradouro da Beira da Quinta, and it's close to Santana.

Some of the nicest views over the Atlantic Ocean and the northern part of Madeira Island can be found from this lovely vantage point. On a clear day, Porto Santo, the nearby island, is even visible. As you travel around the island, don't be afraid to pause and take in this stunning location for a little while.

19. OUR FAVORITE MADERA BEACH IS SEIXAL!

Beaches, sun, cliffs, and vineyards—what more could you want? Yet another lovely place to visit in Madeira is this sleepy little village on the island's north shore. Our favorite beaches on the island are definitely Seixal.

It also becomes a very good novice surfing area when the conditions are right.

20. MIRADOURO DO VÉU DA NOIVA

Madeira's other well-known vantage point is Miradouro do Véu da Noiva.

One of the most exquisite viewpoints on the island of Madeira is Véu da Noiva. From there, you may take in views of the island's north and the stunning waterfall of the same name.

You'll think you're looking at a bride's veil when you see how high the waterfall is and how much water is cascading down the cliff—thus the name.

Situated on the former ER 101 route that linked Seixal and São Vicente, is the viewpoint. It was possible to drive under the waterfall until a few years ago. However, in 2008, a massive landslide destroyed a portion of the road and the tunnel that went beneath the waterfall.

21. PORTO MONIZ, ONE OF MADERA'S MOST VISITED SITES!

On the island's northwest shore sits the quaint tiny village of Porto Moniz. Porto Moniz is unquestionably a must-see location when visiting Madeira and searching for the most picturesque spots. And we soon saw why: the city boasts magnificent lava and rock natural pools. It is a fairly well-known location in Madeira.

Another specialty of Porto Moniz is its fresh seafood cuisine. There are lots of different restaurants close to the natural pools.

22. FANAL AND ITS PERMANENT haze!

Do you enjoy fairy tales and trees? Visit this enchanted forest, where a heavy mist is frequently present.

This feels like the set of a dream movie. We also came across some quite large cows having a good time in the bush. What a beautiful location!

23. FAJÃ DAS ACHADAS DA CRUZ

You may get a great view of Fajã das Achadas da Cruz and the Atlantic Ocean from the Achadas da Cruz viewpoint, which is located in Madeira Island's northwest. There's a cable car (built in 2004) next to the viewpoint that takes you to Fajã das Achadas da Cruz, where you may explore the beach, modest cabins, and farmlands.

24. WATERFALL IN GARGANTA FUNDA

Walk a short distance to the stunning vantage point to witness the Garganta Funda waterfall.

You will be astounded by the area's splendor as soon as you arrive at the viewpoint. The waterfall, which is near the Atlantic Ocean and encircled by cliffs, may be seen from an amazing height.

25. A HIKE ALONG THE 25 FONTES, ONE OF MADERA'S MOST FAMOUS TRAILS

You have to trek at least one Levada when in Madeira! You will not be let down. This is a component of Madeira's spirit.

The Levada das 25 Fontes is a well-known Levada walk that is highly recommended for viewing stunning waterfalls and exquisitely gorgeous native vegetation.

At the conclusion of the trip, you may witness 25 Fontes Waterfall and Risco Waterfall, which flow into a lake.

26. This is our ultimate favorite hike in Madeira: LEVADA DO CALDEIRÃO VERDE!

Situated 980 meters above sea level, directly above the little town of Santana, Levada do Caldeirão Verde is located in the center of the Queimadas Forest Natural Park.

Constructed around the 1700s, the purpose of this levada was to gather water for agriculture from the Caldeirão Verde River.

Levada do Caldeirão Verde is six kilometers in length. The journey will culminate in a breathtaking waterfall. You will pass through tunnels, pass by numerous waterfalls, and take in Madeira's breathtaking scenery throughout the route. A true visual treat, certain spots provide you an unhindered vista and a peek of the ocean.

Our climb up this Levada took us almost the whole day. We brought our lunch and snapped a ton of pictures. Despite the intense rain, it was a memorable experience.

Since the road was extremely damp, we highly advise wearing appropriate hiking shoes!

27. PONTA DO PARGO

Did you ever visit Hawaii? If not, visit Ponta do Pargo, which reminded us a lot of Kauai, Hawaii's Na Pali Coast. To reach the white and red lighthouse, take the Ponta do Pargo route. Beautiful cliffs, wildflowers, and a mesmerizing sunset will all be visible to you.

This is our favorite spot in Madeira!

28. VISIT SAO VICENTE TO SURF.

A well-known location for surfers worldwide is São Vicente. Impressive cliffs and waves may be seen along the coast, along with a few waterfalls by the rocks.

You can also visit some caves in São Vicente. A few hundred thousand years ago, the Paúl da Serra volcano erupted, creating the São Vicente caverns. Its galleries display formations of dried lava, lakes of translucent water, and other sights. The cavities were created as a result of lava flows.

29. JARDIM DO MAR, ANOTHER AMAZING PLACE TO SURF IN MADERA

This quiet fishing village is where surfers get together, and it's located west of Madeira. We loved its charming azulejos, charming little churches, welcoming locals, and stunning views of the beach and mountains.

On the day we visited, though, there were absolutely no waves. Thus, if you plan to go surfing at Jardim do Mar, be sure to check the weather forecast.

30. VISIT PORTO SANTO, A NEIGHBORING ISLAND

Known as the "golden island" due to its 9 kilometres of gorgeous, fine-sand beach, Porto Santo also has other hidden gems that you simply must see. UNESCO designated it as a biosphere reserve in 2020!

The Portuguese discovered the island of Porto Santo, which is 11 km long and 6 km wide, first in the Madeira archipelago in 1418 after being forced to veer off their original course by severe weather.

To travel to Porto Santo, a ferry is required.

CHAPTER 7

Gourmet Delights

You won't go hungry on your first visit to Madeira, so don't worry!

Madeira is fantastic since it offers a wide variety of foods that are specific to the island as well as common Portuguese fare from the mainland.

This isn't a thorough examination; it's just a brief synopsis. That deserves its own post!

Every menu will have Bola da Caco as an appetizer. It's Madeiran garlic bread, but the bread itself is really noteworthy. Made with flour and sweet potatoes, it resembles a cross between crumpets, flatbread, and naan. Please have faith in me. Why not? It's only a few euros everywhere you go.

There is no lack of seafood in Madeira. Lapas, also known as limpets, are typically served as an appetizer (tasting a bit like a tiny, crunchy mussel) with a variety of fish options for the main course. From sea bream to parrotfish to swordfish.

Scabbard fish, however, is the fish that appears on most menus. If you're interested in seeing what a black scabbard fish looks like, I'll let you Google it yourself. It's not pretty. Deep-sea predators like this species are exclusive to deepwater fishing gear.

Typically, the scabbard fish is served with bananas, another delicacy from the area, and occasionally a sauce made of passion fruit. Unquestionably worthwhile to try at least once!

Place an order for espetadas if you'd want to sample meat. Grilled meat served atop skewers. The majority of restaurants will hang the skewers for you in the center of the table.

If there's one reason you should travel to Madeira over the Christmas season, make it carne vinha d'alhos! The pork is marinated in wine and garlic before being sandwiched between Madeira bread. Please don't criticize me; I could eat one of them every day. Although you won't often find it outside of the holidays, if you visit during Christmas, you can find it at every other stall in the markets and fair.

Try the Madeira honey cake, or bolo de mel de cana, if you're craving dessert.

Consider the traditional Madeira wine for your beverages. I would liken it to port because it is quite sweet. All around the island, there are wine samples; some restaurants even host their own wine tastings, although a glass or bottle of wine is always available on the menu.

*Interesting fact: After signing the Declaration of Independence, the founding fathers of America raised a glass of Madeira wine!

Consider trying some poncha if you'd like something fruitier. Fishermen used to sip this VERY powerful beverage, traditionally made with aguardente de cana (sugar cane brandy), honey, sugar, and lemon juice, to stay warm.

These days, each cafe or restaurant has its unique take on poncha. Though it's most frequently seen with passion fruit or orange juice, "traditional" lemon poncha is available everywhere.

I'm just going to warn you once: this stuff is powerful. Do not guzzle it; instead, savor it. A local told me to have one poncha to last you the entire evening, and I think that's about right. Of course, no more than two!

MADERA'S TOP LOCAL DISHES

Onion and Tomato Soup

The tastes of this hot soup are robust and reassuring. Olive oil, fresh tomatoes, diced onions, and garlic are the ingredients. A poached egg sits in the center, offering a place to dip a piece of toast.

Corn-Fried Tuna Steak

One important resource for Madeira's fishing sector is tuna. The tuna in this recipe is sliced, salted, and marinated in a "molho de vilão" sauce. Garlic, oregano, pepper, vinegar, and olive oil are the ingredients of this sauce. After cooking in a skillet, corn flour is cooled on a dish and then sliced into tiny cubes. Local eateries often serve these as a side dish after they've been fried.

Banana with black scabbard—our favorite meal

The elongated fish known as scabbard is only found in a few special locations worldwide, such the open sea off the coast of Madeira, which is roughly 1000 meters deep. Fish enthusiasts will be thrilled with its flavor despite its unattractive appearance. Swordfish fillets are seasoned with salt, pepper, garlic, and lemon juice. After being peeled, the fish fillets and bananas are cooked, dusted with fresh parsley, then dipped in egg and flour. Served with tomato salad, lettuce, and boiled potatoes, known as "semilhas".

Bolo do capo, our daily indulgence!

The traditional bread of Madeira is called bolo do caco, and it is created from sweet potatoes, flour, yeast, water, and salt. This soft stone pan is used to bake sweet bread that has been kneaded into a ball shape and then flattened. Usually, it's served warm with butter made from garlic. Fries, fried corn, and salad are examples of sides. A MATTER OF MADIRA THAT YOU MUST TRY!

Pork with Garlic and Wine

Little pork cubes are marinated and cooked in a mixture of white wine, vinegar, bay leaves, and pepper in this recipe. It is offered in "Bolo do caco" sandwiches or alongside pieces of fried bread. It is particularly well-liked around Christmas.

Pudding with passion fruit

One of the most consumed fruits in Madeira is the passion fruit. There are several varieties of passion fruit, including banana-flavored varieties. The Passiflora edulis is the most prevalent. Its strong perfume, sweet flavor, and varied acidity (based on ripening level) make it the perfect fruit for desserts and regional beverages. Condensed milk, cream, passion fruit pulp, and jelly are the ingredients of passion fruit pudding. Enjoy this remarkable blend of scents.

.

CHAPTER 8

Culture and Heritage

An open-air museum

The Madeiran islands have a diverse architectural heritage of great historical importance. The visit to the cities and towns of this treasure of the Atlantic is enhanced by their monuments.

North Coast

Filled with iconic monuments, the north coast is well worth exploring. Come here to get a true taste of Madeira's culture.

This Atlantic archipelago is undoubtedly a floating garden, and it would be accurate to describe it as a true open-air museum as well.

This is due to the immense worth that the islands' architectural legacy bestows upon their towns and cities' streets.

The monuments of Madeira are a testament to the artistic, architectural, and cultural diversity of six centuries of history.

Casa de Santana

They are, definitely, one of the most outstanding ex-libris of the municipality of Santana. But they developed into much more than that over time.

One of the most recognizable and iconic features of the Madeira archipelago nowadays is the Santana typical house. These unusual structures take us on a genuine historical tour of the island. As a result, the materials used to construct the Casa de Santana are evidence of the resources that were most readily available in the area at the time.

The wood used to construct these triangular-shaped homes is inexpensive and readily available in this area, which aids in maintaining a comfortable interior temperature. Additionally, another method of using grain crops like wheat and rye was the well-known thatched roof. Rainwater could flow from the house because of the roofs' sloping design, which ensured its impermeability.

Even from the exterior, Santana's typical homes are distinguished by their vivid red, blue, and white hues. On the other hand, the interior was limited to a ground floor that was used for household purposes and contained a kitchen and a bedroom, as well as an attic for storing agricultural products.

To find out more about this Madeiran symbol, go to the Núcleo de Casas Típicas de Santana.

Specifics

Casas de Santana, with its distinctive thatched roof and triangular shape, is one of the archipelago's most recognizable sights and a unique piece of historical heritage.

São João Baptista Fort

One of the most popular destinations for tourists visiting this area is the São João Baptista Fort, which is situated in the scenic parish of Porto Moniz on Madeira Island's north coast. Not only is it significant historically, but the Madeira Aquarium is currently housed there.

Replicating the ancient fortification, São João Baptista Fort dates back to 1730. The Porto do Moniz City Council decided to gather the defensive structure's remnants in 1998, and two years later restoration work started with the intention of preserving what was left of the old outer walls and using the local stone to recreate the original 18th-century construction.

The goal of this fort's construction was to defend Porto de Moniz from the pirates' regular raids and pillage during the period. But the São João Baptista Fort has a very different purpose now.

The Madeira Aquarium is situated here. It incorporates twelve demonstration tanks, one of which holds almost half a million liters of salt water. Here, more than ninety indigenous species coexist, reflecting the variety of Madeira's aquatic environments.

Specifics

The São João Baptista Fort is a re-creation of the 1730 original fort. Currently housing the Madeira Aquarium, it is situated in the Porto Moniz parish.

Santa Ana Fountain

The wealthy and extensive archipelago of Madeira has a rich historical and cultural legacy. Numerous monuments adorn towns and cities' streets while also providing historical context. This is the situation with the Santa Ana Fountain, which is situated at Santana on the island's north shore.

Situated in the town center, close to the Santana Parish Church, this spout-adorned building has been recognized by the Regional Department of Cultural Affairs (DRAC) since 2000 as a Monument of Local Value. However, its history predates by several decades.

General Craveiro Lopes, the President of the Republic at the time, dedicated the Santa Ana Fountain in June 1955. It is currently an essential feature of this municipality's architectural environment. When you visit the Santana municipality, don't miss this interesting point of interest, which is composed of exposed stone masonry and plastered with tile panels.

Don't miss the chance to see the Parish Church that is near to this monument. Discover also the ex-libris of the municipality (and one of the hallmarks of the archipelago), the triangular-shaped thatched dwellings that are emblematic of Santana.

Specifics

Situated adjacent to the Santana Parish Church, the Santa Ana Fountain is a feature of the municipality's architectural landscape and has been designated as a Monument of Local Value since 2000.

Fortim do Faial

There is a really unusual location in the Santana municipality that provides visitors with a breathtaking landscape and a trip back in time. Of course, this is the Fortim do Faial viewpoint, one of the must-see locations on Madeira's north shore.

This location, which dates back to the 18th century, has a recreational architectural profile. A historical encroachment enhanced by certain artifacts still in situ, including the ten miniature English-made cannons that had served as the location's defense.

Here, the Fortim do Faial was constructed as a watchtower against potential invasion. With an external wall and a semi-circular layout that matches the slope's profile, the area now serves as a recreation of a military battery. The fort still has an ashlar masonry capstone, and the lower two thirds are better developed.

Because of its unique outlook and popularity as a monument of local value, it has been recognized as such since 1996. Viewpoints of Faial, São Roque do Faial, Porto da Cruz, the majestic Penha d'Águia, and Ponta de São Lourenço can all be seen from the Fortim do Faial. You may even see out the island of Porto Santo on clear days.

Specifics

Constructed in the 18th century as a watchtower against intruders, the Fortim do Faial provides guests with a glimpse into the past along with an expansive vista of Madeira's northern coast.

Biosphere Garden

Madeira's distinct environmental richness has earned it international recognition. The Santana parish is home to the Biosphere Monument, which emphasizes the significance of this legacy.

The Biosphere Garden, a green area established to commemorate and preserve the memory of the significant honor given to the Santana municipality in June 2011—that of being designated as a 'Biosphere Reserve' by UNESCO— incorporates this sculpture. In order to achieve entirely sustainable development, the archipelago's work on biodiversity conservation has received the highest level of international acclaim.

Luís Paixão, a Madeiran artist, created the design, which was unveiled in March 2012. In honoring this natural legacy, the Biosphere Monument seeks to illustrate the healthy coexistence of the Earth and its inhabitants.

Consequently, the Biosphere Monument depicts the relationship between the human being, symbolized by a female figure, and the planet, in its spherical form. The sculpture is based on water, which is an essential component of life. Thus, it is a hymn to upholding moral principles like meticulous respect for the natural world and its biodiversity.

Specifics

The Biosphere Monument in Santana honors the city's designation as a 'Biosphere Reserve,' given by UNESCO. It pays homage to the ecosystems of Madeira's richness.

Faial Old Bridge

The Faial Old Bridge, at 130 meters, was the longest bridge on the island of Madeira for a considerable amount of time. What's left of its massive edifice is now a significant historical site in the area.

This bridge, which was constructed in the early 1900s, was intended to connect the two sides of the parish of Faial, which are divided by the Ribeira do Faial. When it was first opened in 1904, it was the longest on the island. Because of its seven arches, it would subsequently be referred to as the "Bridge of the Seven Mouths".

But in 1984, eighty years after it opened, a powerful storm that struck Madeira's north coast demolished this bridge. Four of the structure's seven arches collapsed because it was unable to withstand the river's roaring surges.

Rebuilding the Faial Old Bridge was abandoned in the wake of this incident. The Primeiro de Julho Bridge was subsequently constructed a short distance away and made accessible to the public in 1986. However, the ancient bridge's three surviving arches have been maintained and are a significant historical landmark in the municipality.

Specifics

The longest bridge on the island of Madeira for a considerable amount of time, the Faial Old Bridge, was damaged by a storm in 1984. Three of its seven arches still stand today.

São Jorge Ruins

Madeira's sugar cane industry began in the fifteenth century. Owing to the rapid rise in importance of this agricultural species in the region, the island rose to prominence as a key European supplier of sugar. Visitors can turn the pages of this history with them when they visit the São Jorge Ruins.

The center of Calhau de São Jorge is made up of the remnants of the former sugar cane mills that were established there during the initial stages of the island's colonization. The remarkably intact pebble entrance portico is the most notable feature of these historic structures.

It should be mentioned that since 2003, the entire São Jorge Ruins in the Santana municipality have been designated as a Monument of Municipal Interest. As such, it is a highly interesting location on the island of Madeira's north shore.

Make sure to utilize this opportunity to experience the breathtaking surroundings that Calhau de São Jorge has to offer. Nestled between verdant hills and the sea, this isolated beach is situated on a tiny freshwater lagoon within the bed of the Ribeira de São Jorge. Come appreciate the history and nature of Madeira!

Specifics

The remains of the sugar cane mills that were constructed at Calhau de São Jorge during the early days of the island's settlement can be found in the São Jorge Ruins.

Any visitor to Funchal can't help but notice the architectural wealth of an archipelago that has been inhabited for more than 600 years.

This island destination offers guests a plethora of opportunities for exploration, discovery, and contemplation, ranging from palaces and statues to fortresses, cathedrals, fountains, shrines, cruises, and theaters. Because of the era in which they were constructed as well as global artistic influences, Madeira's monuments are incredibly varied. Throughout its secular historical journey, this significant cultural asset has been constructed to serve a variety of purposes.

Funchal Cathedral

Funchal Cathedral, which has been recognized as a National Monument since 1910, has a significant role in the history, geography, and daily life of the city. Admired by many for its unparalleled historical, architectural, and artistic significance, this is the primary religious church of the Madeira archipelago.

King D. João II ordered the first construction of this monument in 1493. Completed during the beginning of the 16th century, it exhibits Gothic and Manueline style characteristics. On its façade, for instance, is a magnificent

Gothic portal made of Cabo Girão sandstone that has eight archivolts arranged in a pointed arch.

The altarpiece inside the Funchal Cathedral immediately grabs one's attention. It is a massive polyptych with gilded woodcarving, topped by a Gothic canopy, and is accompanied by sculptures and oil paintings on wood. An examination of the ceiling is also recommended. It is a magnificent example of Mudéjar décor, or alfarje ceilings from the Islamic artistic heritage, and was worked in cedar from the island.

The Funchal Cathedral's creative legacy does not end there, though. This monument has not only the ornate chancel chair in the main chapel but also a processional cross that is regarded as one of the masterworks of Portuguese Manueline jewelry.

ADDRESS

Funchal, Rua do Aljube, 9000-067

07:15–18:30 Monday–Friday; 08:00–12:00 Saturday; 16:00–19:00 Sunday; 07:15–12:00 | 16:00–19:00

(+351 291 228 155,)

catedraldofunchal@gmail.com

https://www.catedraldofunchal.com

Specifics

The main religious building in Madeira, Funchal Cathedral is located in the city's historic center and has a legacy of unparalleled importance. It showcases elements of the Manueline and Gothic periods.

Mercado dos Lavradores

Madeira is well-known for its superior local goods, partly because of the exceptionally fertile soils and subtropical climate the island enjoys. The Mercado dos Lavradores, a major landmark in the heart of Funchal, is a living museum that puts the flavors of the archipelago's freshness, vibrancy, and tropicality front and center.

The opening of this business area took place on November 24, 1940. The Mercado dos Lavradores has now become a regular feature of Funchal residents' daily lives. For tourists visiting the island, it has also turned into a must as they immerse themselves in a lively and exuberant atmosphere.

The structure features characteristic Estado Novo architecture, designed by Edmundo Tavares. The Mercado dos Lavradores was intended to be the city's main supply hub, as seen by its size and location. Large tile panels from 1940, painted with regional motifs by João Rodrigues, from the Faience Battistini plant in Maria de Portugal, adorn the façade, the entrance door, and the fishmonger's store.

The variety of hues, scents, individuals, and tastes that define this Madeira market set it apart. Come explore it!

ADDRESS

Largo dos Lavradores | Funchal, 9060-158

07:00 - 19:00 Monday through Thursday; 07:00 - 20:00 Friday; 07:00 - 14:00 Saturday; Closed on Sunday

(+351 291 214 080)

Specifics

The city's supply hub, the Mercado dos Lavradores, was opened in 1949 in the heart of Funchal. The most well-known fresh and tropical goods from the Madeira archipelago can be found here.

The Convent of Santa Clara

The Convent of Santa Clara, which dates to the late fifteenth century, is a remarkable example of the historical legacy that enhances Funchal. It was once a part of a closed religious order but is now accessible to the public.

Situated atop Calçada de Santa Clara, this structure was constructed between 1489 and 1496 at the behest of João Gonçalves da Câmara, the second captain-donee of Funchal. These buildings were built with the intention of housing the girls of the local nobility at the time.

The Convent of Santa Clara in Funchal is a collection of buildings of outstanding artistic and architectural merit. It has seventeenth-century Hispano-Arabic tiles on its walls. The ceilings are then crafted from wood. A collection of repaired canvases from the 17th and 18th centuries is also kept in these facilities.

The São Gonçalo de Amarante Chapel, which is believed to have been constructed in the 16th century, the atrium, the porch leading to the choirs and the Gothic cloister, the Coro de Baixo and the Coro de Cima, may all be seen when visiting the Convent of Santa Clara. Finally, spend some time touring the Santa Clara Church, which the island's discoverer, João Gonçalves Zarco, commissioned.

ADDRESS

Santa Clara 15 Football Club | 9000-036 Funchal

10:00–12:30 | 14:00–17:00, Tuesday–Saturday

(+351 291 145 330)

Specifics

At the close of the fifteenth century, the Santa Clara Convent was constructed in Funchal. This collection of ecclesiastical structures has a great deal of historical and artistic significance.

Fortress of São Tiago

The History of Funchal documents corsair invasions that have occurred repeatedly over the ages. Some forts, like the Fortress of São Tiago, were constructed with the intention of forming an efficient defensive belt to safeguard the city's integrity. These days, it is a well-liked travel destination.

This castle, which dates back to the early 17th century, is positioned advantageously above the waterfront of the city's ancient Zona Velha (Old Town). Under the direction of the royal master builder Reais Jerónimo Jorge, work on it started in the middle of 1614. Bartolomeu João, his son, finished it later.

The Fortress of São Tiago has undergone numerous restorations over the ages. Furthermore, this military-style urban fort served a variety of functions over the years, including housing flood victims in 1803, headquarters for British troops or the Army Police, and the 1992 installation of the Contemporary Art Museum (which was moved to the Casa das Mudas in Calheta in 2015).

Presently, guests have the chance to go through Madeira's history at the Fortress of São Tiago, while enjoying an exclusive vista of the Atlantic.

Specifics

Situated above the waterfront in the Zona Velha, the Fortress of São Tiago dates back to the early 17th century and was built to protect Funchal against corsair invasions.

São José Fort

São José Fort, which was constructed to guard Funchal's sea entry, is now a highly significant site of significance. A visit to this monument should be part of any tour of Madeira's capital because of its historical significance and the expansive view of the Atlantic it provides.

The "Ilhéu de São José" is a rock formation upon which this stronghold is perched. According to history, this is where the island of Madeira, which was then covered in a thick layer of vegetation, was hidden when João Gonçalves Zarco and Tristão Vaz Teixeira, the discoverers, arrived.

Later, São José Fort was constructed here in the middle of the eighteenth century. It should be mentioned that, considering the importance of the port of Funchal in international trade at the time, fortifying the city's defensive infrastructures was imperative. However, this fort ended up acting as the invaders' headquarters and afterwards as a prison while British troops occupied Madeira between 1801 and 1807.

The building had a long-standing undervaluation. Nonetheless, the private individual who purchased Forte de São José was inspired to revitalize this area by its indisputable historical, architectural, and cultural significance.

Specifics

According to history, the islet on which São José Fort was constructed in the eighteenth century served as the first refuge used by the island's discoverers.

São João Baptista Fort

One of the Island of Madeira's features is São João Batista Fort, popularly referred to as "Pico Fort," which is located 111 meters above sea level. With its breathtaking view of the Atlantic, this landmark is a must-see among the many things to do in Funchal.

This fortification was constructed in the 17th century with the intention of strengthening the city's defenses against the regular pirate invasions. In the early going, it functioned as the city's gunpowder stockpile, meant for all the forts and towers on the island, in addition to being a privileged surveillance position.

The São João Batista Fort was given to the Navy in the middle of the 20th century, and the Navy Communications Center was established there. Once the fortress was occupied by the Naval Radio Telegraphic Station of Funchal, multiple antennae were visible. The locals started referring to the city as "Pico Rádio" (Radio Peak) as a result.

A number of renovation interventions have lately been made to the São João Batista Fort. As a result, it now has a multipurpose space for conferences or concerts as well as a restaurant where guests can relax and take in the stunning view of Funchal.

Specifics

Constructed during the 17th century with the intention of fortifying Funchal's defense, the renowned São João Batista Fort provides one of the most exclusive sweeping views of Funchal.

Historic Center of Santo Amaro - Torre do Capitão

The island of Madeira's rich architectural legacy reflects its history, which dates back several centuries to the time of its discovery. The earliest surviving example of civil building in the archipelago can be seen at the Santo Amaro Historic Centre - Torre do Capitão.

This area, which is in the parish of Santo António's Caminho de Santo Amaro, is home to a collection of noteworthy structures that date from the fifteenth to the eighteenth century. The Torre do Capitão, the Santo Amaro Chapel, the Casa dos Romeiros, and a newly built structure with a technical area and a space for temporary exhibitions are the four buildings.

The mid-15th-century Torre do Capitão, which has elements of medieval architecture, was constructed by Garcia Homem de Sousa, João Gonçalves Zarco's son-in-law. Conversely, the Santo Amaro Chapel, which dates back to the fifteenth century, has an equally impressive collection. Two of the collection's highlights are the altar, sculpted by Rui Sanches, and a Pedro Calapez stained glass window.

Lastly, visitors to the area for the celebrations honoring Santo Amaro were once welcomed at the Casa dos Romeiros. Now undergoing renovations, this structure serves as the Santo Amaro Historic Center's shop and welcome area.

ADDRESS

Funchal, Caminho Santo Amaro, 9020-121

10:00–12:00 and 14:00–17:00 on Monday through Friday; closed on Saturday, Sunday, and public holidays.

(291 941-641 378 | (291 946-342 281)

Specifics

Situated in the upper region of Funchal municipality, the Santo Amaro Historic Centre - Torre do Capitão is home to some of the oldest examples of civic architecture in the Madeira archipelago.

City Hall of Funchal

The Funchal City Council holds a prominent position within the municipality. Funchal City Hall is currently housed in this historically significant and very architecturally valuable palace in the city, which still maintains its original layout.

This old edifice unquestionably defines the urban environment in the bustling city center. It was constructed in 1758 to house the Count of Carvalhal. It then went through a number of owners and tenants before the City Council bought it in 1883. After then, it became Funchal's City Hall.

Through the years, it has undergone renovations and modifications, but its features have remained constant. As so, it is a well-balanced example of late eighteenth-century architecture. The inner planted courtyard with Battistini tiles, completed in 1940 at the Maria de Portugal Factory, and the fountain adorned with a marble statue of "Leda and the Swan," autographed by Germano José Salles, are the most notable features of these structures.

Weekday tours of this historic structure are available to the public in multiple languages. In just sixty minutes, this is the ideal approach to discover the beauties of Funchal City Hall.

ADDRESS

Funchal, Praça do Município, 9004-512

11:00 on Monday through Friday; closed on Saturday, Sunday, and on public holidays

(+351) 291 705 060 (tours guided)

Constructed in 1758, the iconic palace that houses the Town Hall has managed to preserve its original design, making it a well-balanced representation of late eighteenth-century architecture.

S. Lourenço Palace, the most striking example of military and civic architecture on the Island of Madeira, is a must-see. It is situated in a key location for defense of Funchal.

The early part of the 16th century saw the start of this historic building's construction. It was finished between 1580 and 1640, during the Spanish dynasty's rule over Portugal. It was mostly focused on a defensive operation in the initial instance. Afterwards, it was to serve as the captain-general governors' and captains-donee of Funchal's home.

When the constitutional government was established in 1834, S. Lourenço Palace, the Fortress of S. Without a doubt, Lourenço was assigned a residential role. Two years later, it was split into two areas: the Military Area, which houses the Madeira Military Zone Command, and the Palace, which serves as the official residence of the Civil Governor. There was also a museum with an extensive collection of armaments.

In 1943, S. Lourenço Palace was designated as a National Monument. Considering the modifications it has experienced throughout the years, its architecture blends military, Manueline, and Mannerist elements. It serves as the Representative of the Republic's official residence today.

ADDRESS

Zarco Avenue | 9001–902 Funchal

Monday at 12:30; Tuesday and Wednesday at 10:00; Thursday at 10:00; Friday at 3:00; Saturday and Sunday closed.

(651 92 202 530)

Specifics

The commencement of S's construction. The palace in Lourenço is sixteenth-century in age. Erected in 1943 and designated as a National Monument, it stands as the most formidable representation of Madeira's military and civil architecture.

The Regional Government Palace

The Regional Government Palace, situated in the bustling heart of Madeira's capital, dominates the cityscape. This remarkable edifice, which is located on Avenida Arriaga, one of Funchal's most significant and historic thoroughfares, is significant to the history of the city.

This palace's oldest section was constructed in the late 17th century on the location of the Funchal Medical School. The

Misericórdia of Funchal and its hospital were housed there at the time of its construction, which was done for humanitarian purposes.

Over the years, the structure experienced numerous alterations and served a variety of purposes. The Regional Executive had already acquired control of the facilities before the end of the 20th century. As such, it was eventually transformed into the Regional Government Palace and served as the home of multiple Regional Secretariats.

A tour of the Regional Government Palace enables us to discover a number of interesting ornamental aspects that transport us back to that historical period, despite the structure having undergone multiple restructurings that have gradually stripped it of its original 17th-century features. This is the situation with the original 17th-century polychrome tile panels that adorn this area.

Specifics

Constructed around the close of the 1700s to accommodate the city's Misericórdia and Hospital, this edifice is presently serving as the Regional Government Palace, housing multiple Regional Secretariats.

The Shrine of Nossa Senhora da Paz

The Shrine of Nossa Senhora da Paz is the largest monument on the Island of Madeira, both symbolically and physically. On August 14, the Day of Nossa Senhora do Monte, it was officially opened as a result of a pledge given by the Madeiran people.

Dedicated to Nossa Senhora da Paz, this artwork is located in Terreiro da Luta, in the parish of Monte. It is signed by architect Emanuel Ribeiro. This tale of loyalty takes us back to 1917, when German submarines twice bombarded the city of Funchal during World War I.

A pledge was then made in response to these occurrences: the Madeirans would build a statue in honor of Senhora do Monte if peace was restored to the island. Ten years after these incidents, the shrine dedicated to Nossa Senhora da Paz was constructed, with a five-meter-tall marble statue.

There's an odd rosary at the foot of the Shrine of Nossa Senhora da Paz. The chains from the ships that were sunk during the raids were used to construct this symbolic element. As such, it is a unique monument that is well worth a thorough examination and is located in the higher region of the municipality of Funchal.

Specifics

The Madeirans made a pledge during the 1917 bombing of Funchal, which led to the creation of the marble shrine known as the Shrine of Nossa Senhora da Paz in the Monte parish.

Teatro Baltazar Dias

Cultural Program

The Teatro Municipal Baltazar Dias is a monument of considerable relevance, whose elegance is quite noticeable in the city center of Funchal. It serves as the stage for an important part of the city's active cultural life. Not only is this venue valuable historically and architecturally, but its programming is also worth getting to know.

For a large portion of the 19th century, the Madeirans demanded that a new theater be built in Funchal following the destruction of the Teatro Grande in 1833. On March 11, 1888, this new location would finally have its formal opening. Constructed to resemble the Italian model, it was modeled after the São Carlos Theatre in Lisbon and the La Scala Theatre in Milan.

After utilizing several aliases, such as "D". Maria Pia, "Doctor" The theater was originally known as "Teatro Funchalense" or "Manuel de Arriaga," but as times changed, it was renamed "Teatro Municipal Baltazar Dias" in 1935 to honor the blind poet and dramatist who was born in Madeira in the sixteenth century.

The Baltazar Dias Municipal Theatre is a work of architectural beauty in and of itself. Its equilibrium is enhanced by the decoration and scenography created by two renowned artists, Portuguese Eugénio do Nascimento Cotrim and Italian Luigi Manini. It now serves as a point of reference for Portuguese culture.

ADDRESS

Funchal, Avenida Arriaga, 9000-060

09:00 - 12:30 on Monday and Tuesday; 14:00 - 17:30 on Wednesday and Thursday; 09:00 - 21:30 on Friday; and 13:30 - 21:30 on Saturday and Sunday.

teatro.baltazardias@funchal.pt/

funchal.pt/teatrobaltazardias/

Specifics

The Baltazar Dias Municipal Theatre was built in 1888 and features a classically Italian architectural style that is attractive and well-balanced. It occupies a significant position in Funchal's cultural life.

Toilets that are adapted; stair climbers that enable entry to the building by stairs; a Braille visit guide; a lowered ticket counter; a 3D model of the building; two wheelchair-accessible spots in the performance space.

Eastern Seaboard

Discover locations rich in history and learn more about the cultural legacy of the towns of Machico and Santa Cruz.

As a result, the archipelago is home to forts that were constructed to defend the populace from corsair attacks, palaces with lush gardens that catered to the needs of the passing European aristocracy, and statues and busts honoring some of the key figures and events in Madeiran history.

Tristão Vaz Teixeira Statue

The entire population of the archipelago cherishes the history of Madeira's discovery because of the courage and audacity needed to make it. For this reason, the memorial of Tristão Vaz Teixeira has great symbolic significance for all Madeirans.

In 1419, Bartolomeu Perestrelo, João Gonçalves Zarco, and navigator Tristão Vaz Teixeira made the arrival on the island of Madeira. They were more than just explorers; they actively participated in the ensuing colonization effort. As a result, they played a crucial part in this Atlantic pearl's social, economic, and cultural development.

In Machico, the statue of Tristão Vaz Teixeira can be found in Largo da Igreja Matriz. The fact that this discoverer was named the first Captain-Donee of Machico makes this municipality's decision to house the monument noteworthy. In 1440, Infante D. Henrique issued a charter granting him authority over this province.

The reason why Madeirans still have such high regard for this man is due to his pivotal role in the archipelago's history. As a result, Tristão Vaz Teixeira's statue was unveiled in 1972 and is now a major feature of the city center. Anjos Teixeira, a Portuguese sculptor, sculpted it in bronze.

Specifics

This Madeira discoverer is honored by a statue in the city of Machico, dedicated to Tristão Vaz Teixeira. Anjos Teixeira created the bronze sculpture, which was unveiled in 1972.

São Fernando Fort

São Fernando Fort is a historically significant landmark situated in the Santa Cruz parish on the east coast of the Island of Madeira. It provides important evidence of the archipelago's historical defense tactics.

Situated advantageously with a view of Santa Cruz Beach is the São Fernando Fort. Because of its location, possible threats to the region's defense might be promptly observed. It should be mentioned that corsair invasions were a long-standing threat to Madeira. Such fortifications played a crucial part in keeping the populace safe.

This was the fort built in the eighteenth century. It was eventually restored during the liberal fights by sergeant-major Paulo Dias de Almeida, and it was dubbed 'São Fernando Fort' because an old chapel honoring this saint used to stand on this location. Records from 1820 show that this little church had closed; instead, the guardhouse was located next to a chapel honoring Saint Lazarus, which is also no longer in existence.

Make the most of your time at São Fernando Fort to learn about the rich history of Santa Cruz, a city that is only 18 kilometers from Funchal.

Specifics

São Fernando Fort was constructed in the 18th century to protect this area's shoreline and is situated above Santa Cruz Beach.

Reis Magos Fort

Nestled amidst picturesque surroundings, the Reis Magos Fort is a historically and aesthetically significant landmark. As a result, it is strongly recommended that travelers visiting the Island of Madeira's west coast make a stop there.

The Reis Magos Fort is situated in the Caniço parish, close to a popular tourist destination with a high concentration of lodging. The fort is situated adjacent to Reis Magos Beach, which is well-known for its exceptional water quality. Its annual Blue Flag exhibition is evidence of this.

Constructed during a period of high frequency raids by pirates and corsairs, the Reis Magos Fort performed the vital duty of defending the local inhabitants in this coastal region for several decades. Built in the 18th century, it is a quadrangular construction with a terrace facing the sea and guard stations facing land.

Utilize this fort's opportunity to educate yourself about the region's unparalleled riches of environmental heritage. The Garajau Partial Nature Reserve is a wildlife lover's paradise located nearby.

Specifics

Constructed in the 18th century, the Reis Magos Fort served as a coastal defense. It is surrounded by Reis Magos Beach and has stunning scenery.

Christ the King statue in Garajau

One of the most famous structures on the east coast of Madeira is the statue of Christ the King of Garajau, which is located in one of the most unexpected locations. It is a must-see, attracting tourists with its distinct landscape backdrop.

In honor of the Sagrado Coração de Jesus, a statue of Christ the King of Garajau was built. It is located in the Santa Cruz municipality at the Ponta do Garajau viewpoint. Aires de Ornelas, son of Caniço's last majorat, provided the funding and oversaw the monument's construction. It was officially inaugurated on October 30, 1927. Additionally, that day saw the opening of the road that leads from the village of Cancela to the Monument.

French sculptor Georges Serraz created the design for the Christ the King of Garajau statue. It's a massive sculpture of Jesus Christ facing the Atlantic Ocean with his arms extended; his size inevitably distorts the surrounding landscape.

The Garajau Partial Nature Reserve includes this area. As a result, you may take in the vibrant biodiversity and crystal-clear waters of this protected area. A portion of Funchal Bay can also be seen from the Christ the King observatory.

Specifics

In 1927, the Christ the King of Garajau statue was built. This massive artwork is part of a vantage point from which you can observe the riotous Garajau Partial Nature Reserve.

The Saint Mary of the Mountains

For numerous centuries, Santa Casa da Misericórdia, which is situated in the town of Santa Cruz on the east coast of the Island of Madeira, has been an important social center. It's also worth getting to know the historically significant building that houses this institution.

The Santa Casa da Misericórdia de Santa Cruz structure, which was constructed starting in 1530, is an example of Mannerist hospital architecture. It has undergone multiple modifications. Its rectangular layout includes multiple bodies as well as multiple gardened sections.

Despite significant remodeling throughout the years, the side spaces still have two portals with balcony windows on top of them. The Santa Isabel Chapel is a modest church that is attached to the Santa Casa da Misericórdia de Santa Cruz. It was built in 1562 by the merchant André Gonçalves. It's worth a visit not only for its Gothic doorway but also to take in the gilded woodcarving of its main altar.

Furthermore mentioned is the fact that the Santa Casa da Misericórdia has long offered vital medical and humanitarian services that are vital to the community's health and well-being. Its relationship to the community still matters a lot today.

ADDRESS

9100-161 Santa Cruz | Rua Irmã Wilson 2/6

(291 524 190) +351)

scmstacruz@hotmail.com

Santa Cruz, Misericordia

Specifics

The sixteenth-century edifice that houses the Santa Casa da Misericórdia de Santa Cruz features Mannerist hospital architecture. This organization is vital to society.

Sister Mary Jane Wilson's sculpture

A number of individuals hold a particular place in the hearts of the islanders and will always be remembered in the pages of Madeira's history. The sculpture by Sister Mary Jane Wilson honors one of these remarkable individuals.

This group of sculptures is located in the serene Santa Cruz Municipal Garden, which is surrounded by the colors of nature in the heart of the city. Sculpted by Luís Paixão, the piece debuted in February 2014.

This figure, who arrived in Madeira in 1881, is thus honored by the sculpture of Sister Mary Jane Wilson (1840–1916). She came to the island as a nurse traveling with an English patient, but she ended up remaining in Funchal and remained there for the remainder of her life.

She established the Congregation of the Franciscan Sisters of Our Lady of Victories as early as 1884. She assumed the moniker Sister Mary of St. Francis and committed her life to teaching young people and tending to the ill and impoverished. Thus, Sister Mary Jane Wilson's sculpture serves as a fitting memorial to this person, who the Madeiranos lovingly referred to as "Good Mother".

Specifics

In the Santa Cruz Municipal Gardens, a sculpture honoring Sister Mary Jane Wilson, the founder of the Congregation of the Franciscan Sisters of Our Lady of Victories, was unveiled in 2014.

The Santa Cruz Courthouse

Situated in a peaceful, planted plaza, the Santa Cruz Court Building is a monumental structure that holds significance from both an architectural and historical perspective.

The Santa Cruz Court Building, situated in Largo do Município at the city's entrance, is an unmissable landmark in the urban environment. It was constructed in 1932 to replace the Santa Cruz Court's previous buildings, which had been completely destroyed by fire in 1928.

The Santa Cruz Court building is distinguished by Estado Novo architectural lines, which portray a somber and monumental design, given the historical era in which it was constructed.

The Santa Cruz municipality's coat of arms is displayed on the building's main façade. It has three stories and a rectangular layout as well. The upper two stories have two balconies that span the whole main façade. The eight window slits are arranged in a straight lintel on the side panels.

It is especially noteworthy that the Santa Cruz Court building is encircled by a vibrantly colored garden, with the tropical silk floss tree (Chorisia speciosa) taking center stage.

Specifics

The original courthouse, which burned down in 1928, was replaced with the Santa Cruz Court Building, which was constructed in 1932. Its architecture is typified by Estado Novo characteristics.

Cross Santa Cruz

There are several powerfully symbolic occasions in Madeira's history. The Santa Cruz Cross is a precise representation of one of those legendary moments that have become ingrained in this Atlantic archipelago's collective memory.

Now let's go back to the discovery of Madeira in the fifteenth century. In the midst of the thick forest that covered the entire coastal region at the time, navigator João Gonçalves Zarco discovered ancient cedar trees, using which he had a cross built. 'Santa Cruz' was the new name given to this town on Madeira Island's east coast after this incident.

The Santa Cruz Cross, which is situated in the town's main square, is directly related to this baptismal event. As a result, it has a strong connection to the municipality's toponymy, signifying the wooden cross that the discoverer had built upon landing in the bay.

The Santa Cruz Cross is made consisting of a base with three steps supporting a column made of white marble. It also features a 19th-century crucifix supported by a capital. Despite its metaphorical meaning, it's also vital to remember that this cross is depicted on the town's coat of arms.

Specifics

The Santa Cruz Cross pays respect to the wooden cross that João Gonçalves Zarco placed here upon his landing, consisting of a crucifix, a capital, and a column made of white marble.

Santa Cruz City Council

There are numerous monuments along the east coast of the Island of Madeira that are well worth a detailed inspection. One of them is undoubtedly the Santa Cruz City Council building, which has significant historical and architectural significance.

During the process of colonizing this Atlantic pearl, the municipality of Santa Cruz played an important role. According to history, the place was named in the fifteenth century after the pioneer João Gonçalves Zarco discovered ancient cedars among the thick forest that covered it. He used these cedars to order the construction of a cross.

Originally constructed in the early 16th century, the Santa Cruz City Council building has seen numerous additions and renovations throughout the years. Presently, it showcases modern civil architecture, residential building from the 16th century, and both.

Some of the stylistic characteristics of Santa Cruz City Council, which is located in the town center close to the Mother Church and the Santa Casa da Misericórdia, make it stand out. This is the case with its main door and twinned windows, which are crowned with D's coat of arms. Manuel, in the Manneline-Gothic style.

Specifics

Situated in the town center, the Santa Cruz City Council is an authentic sixteenth-century structure featuring Gothic-Manueline architectural components mixed with sixteenth-century domestic architecture.

Coast of West

When visiting the west coast, make sure not to overlook these two significant structures.

So make sure to take some time to reflect quietly on this unique legacy. The monuments of Madeira provide a living history of the archipelago.

São Bento da Ribeira Brava Fort

Constructed during an era marked by frequent invasions by pirates and corsairs, the São Bento da Ribeira Brava Fort holds significant value in the historical legacy of Madeira's western coast. In order to safeguard the coast and the anchorage, Madeira's governor, Duarte Sodré Pereira, ordered the construction of this fortification in 1708.

Nevertheless, the island's October 1803, flood would ultimately leave the São Bento da Ribeira Brava Fort completely destroyed due to extensive damage. In 1916, over a century later, renovations to this structure started. The monument that is currently on display at the town of Ribeira Brava's waterfront is the outcome of that recovery procedure.

It's a little round tower with a guardhouse situated on a terrace. The gateway with a cement masonry frame in a perfect round arch, topped by an inscription and the national coat of arms, is the focal point of the main façade, which faces north. On the other hand, a little alcove in the São Bento da Ribeira Brava Fort overlooks the sea and features a picture of Saint Benedict. Currently, a tourist information office is located there.

Specifics

In order to defend the coast against corsair invasions, the São Bento da Ribeira Brava Fort was constructed in 1708. The tourist information office is currently located in this ancient structure.

Solar dos Herédia

Solar dos Herédia, Ribeira Brava, has been recognized as a Monument of Municipal Interest since 1994 and is an important part of the island of Madeira's west coast's architectural and historical legacy.

The town center is where you may find this famous Ribeira Brava structure. Francisco Correia Herédia, the Viscount of Ribeira Brava and the municipality's founder, lived there.

Indeed, Solar dos Herédia, Ribeira Brava, has a history spanning over two centuries.

It was constructed sometime in the late 18th and early 19th centuries, and it still has some of the palaces' traditional architectural elements. A sizable outdoor garden that can house a wide variety of plant species is another feature of the facilities.

The town hall's headquarters have been at Solar dos Herédia, Ribeira Brava, since the 1980s. Spend as much time as possible at this place of interest exploring the neighboring São Bento Church, the major church of the parish.

This 16th-century temple boasts Baroque, Mannerist, and Manueline architectural elements. Its interior is filled with an extensive collection of sculptures, paintings, goldsmithing, and gilded woodcarvings.

Specifics

The construction of Solar dos Herédia, Ribeira Brava, took place in the late 1700s and early 1800s. It is designated as a Monument of Municipal Interest due to the richness of its historical and cultural legacy.

Porto Santo

When you go down the Porto Santo pier, keep an eye out for a significant monument.

Padrão dos Descobrimentos

It is inevitable that components from this age will be present on an island with a history of maritime development. The Padrão dos Descobrimentos at Vila Baleira is unquestionably one of these landmarks.

This monument is located on Alameda do Infante, close to the Porto Santo Promenade's historic pier. The locals call it "Pau de Sabão," which translates to "soap stick". Its shape, which was derived from many quadrangular basaltic parts that combine to form an impressive tower, gave rise to its name.

There are reliefs on each side of this square parallelepiped that reference the figures and events of maritime development. Thus, names from this historical period are included in it, as Infante D. Henrique.

Notably, the sculpture has the signature of António Aragão, a prominent figure in Madeiran culture during the 20th century. The official opening was held on August 28, 1960.

Once you've seen this monument, you should definitely explore Vila Baleira's premier green space, the Infante D. Henrique Avenue Garden. After that, take a leisurely stroll down the Porto Santo Promenade and take in the peace and quiet that the sea has to offer.

Specifics

A monument known as Padrão dos Descobrimentos highlights Porto Santo's historical ties to the Portuguese era of maritime expansion. It is located on Infante's Alameda.

Statue of Cristóvío Colombo

The history of Porto Santo includes Christopher Columbus, to the point where the island's museum, Casa Colombo - Museu do Porto Santo, bears his name.

 Nonetheless, the Cristóvão Colombo Statue, another site of significance, has this connection.

Crafted by Madeiran artist Ricardo Veloza, this bust is situated in the Infante D. Henrique Avenue Garden near the center of Vila Baleira.

It was constructed in 1989 as a memorial to the navigator who spent some time living in the Madeira archipelago and was first involved in the sugar trade.

Subsequently, he wed Filipa de Moniz, the daughter of Bartolomeu Perestrelo, the first donee captain of Porto Santo.

The union happened in Lisbon around 1479 or 1480.

Following that, Christopher Columbus is said to have been in Madeira between 1480 and 1482.

It's regarded as a crucial period for his nautical education.

During that period, Porto Santo served as a technical halt for expeditions related to maritime development.

During his third voyage to America in 1498, Christopher Columbus paid a visit to the island.

Owing to its historical significance, the navigator has endured as a highly prevalent reference in the area.

Specifics The Cristóvão Colombo Statue, located in the Infante D. Henrique Avenue Garden in the heart of Vila Baleira, is a conspicuous representation of the navigator's significance in the history of the island.

CHAPTER 9

Realistic Advice

Are you having trouble making travel plans to Madeira? Well, that's not necessary!

Independent travel to Madeira is not difficult. You don't have to purchase an off-the-shelf comprehensive trip package in order to visit Madeira because lodging, transportation, and activities can all be conveniently reserved online. Alternatively, you are free to travel in Madeira as per your own schedule.

At least practically speaking, it doesn't really matter where you choose to stay on the island because it is small. Rarely are the driving distances longer than an hour or so.

The precise processes to organize your trip to Madeira are as follows:

1. Decide when to leave.

Certain places have a certain "best time to visit" or a low season with unquestionably bad weather. This is not the case in Madeira, where year-round pleasant weather prevails.

This is caused by both its exposure to an Atlantic breeze and its subtropical climate. All year round, ocean temperatures range from 18 °C to 24 °C.

Unsurprisingly, July and August continue to be the busiest travel months. It will be the busiest and sunniest time of day.

You can still get lots of sunlight and ideal hiking and outdoor conditions in months like April, May, June, and September.

As temperatures in Madeira often approach 20 °C, winter there feels more like spring on the European mainland. On the other hand, the wettest months of the year are October through February.

In the end, there's never a bad time to visit Madeira, so schedule your vacation whenever it's most convenient for you!

2. Choose the duration of your stay.

We believe two weeks is the perfect amount of time for a first-time visitor to Madeira, particularly if you enjoy exploring, doing road excursions, and having lots of free time for activities.

If you stay in Madeira for less than a week, you won't have enough time to see some of the highlights and have a nice experience. There will be a very limited number of visitors who may come for just one day (from cruise ships) or a few days (during the weekend from Portugal).

The island is not very small, but it is not tiny either. There are lots of sites to explore, and driving from one side to the other still takes around 90 minutes.

Extended visits lasting a month or longer are also available. The island has recently come to the attention of remote workers and digital nomads.

3. Locate your Madeira travel plans.

It's most likely that you will be traveling by airline to Madeira, unless you chance to be coming by cruise ship.

Madeira has excellent connections to locations throughout Europe. Additionally, there is a rare direct trip to New York.

4. Remain in Funchal, or leave.

If this is your first time visiting Madeira, the natural place to base yourself is in the capital, Funchal.

There are the most lodging, dining, transportation, and other alternatives in Funchal0. While based in Funchal, renting a car or having a tour pick you up from your hotel is simple. While traveling to different regions of the island for day trips, you can get about Funchal on foot, by taxi, or through ride-sharing.

A historic fort, cobblestone streets, and a marina can be found in Funchal's compact old center. It also features more contemporary neighborhoods, such as Lido's hotel sector, where you can quickly locate a cozy resort hotel with a pool.

But Funchal, the island's commercial center, is also a heavily populated and bustling neighborhood. If you'd like be in a more tranquil area nearer to nature, this might not be your first option.

In this instance, we suggest making reservations at a hotel, villa, or bed and breakfast in a smaller village or town near the ocean. Think about locations like Machico, Sao Vicente, Ponta do Sol, or Calheta.

5. Choose whether to stay at several locations.

This case for dividing your time between several lodgings may not be as compelling in Madeira, as the majority of locations are only a short drive away (around an hour). Additionally, you should definitely avoid packing a lot or moving around a lot if you're traveling with your family to Madeira.

If you want to make things easy, book a single place to stay for the duration of your journey.

If you're adaptable, though, you might choose to stay in multiple locations. You may spend a week in Madeira's sunnier south and a week in its greener, lusher north, for instance. Alternatively, you may spend most of your time in Funchal and then make a side excursion to Porto Santo, a smaller island that is well-known for its sandy beaches.

6. Think about if you'll require an automobile.

If the most of your time is spent relaxing by the beach or pool, you may get away with just scheduling a few tours to do some sightseeing. But renting a car is by far the finest way to see Madeira in its entirety.

Public transportation can be used to get to some locations, however since the buses are meant for locals, they usually stop at major cities rather than the tourist destinations. To secure the best deal on the vehicle type of your choice, it is worthwhile to reserve your rental car in advance. Make sure to use Discover Cars to look through all the rental businesses and find the best offers. We always reserve our cars in Madeira (or wherever else) through this portal.

7. Observe the weather

Due to its location in the middle of the ocean, numerous mountain peaks, and various microclimates, Madeira experiences erratic weather.

Compared to places like the Azores, where you might frequently experience four seasons in a single day, it is not nearly as intense. Though they can still be very localized, the weather in Madeira is more stable.

It could be a good idea to check the weather before heading to the island's greener north, as rain is more likely to fall there. Hiking the center peaks of the island might become more challenging when there is cloud cover.

We advise checking the weather before you leave and packing with a little flexibility for your vacation. Since they only average the weather throughout the island, Google and Apple weather are not the greatest. Alternatively, to see the actual circumstances in several locations, you might want to visit the island's webcams.

8. Find out what has to be done.

It is beneficial to arrive to the island prepared because there is a lot to do!

We intend to ultimately go into great length about every activity in Madeira on our site, but for now, here are a few to add to your list:

Embark on a cable car journey. There is one that leads to the botanical gardens in Funchal. Beaches at the base of sheer cliffs can be reached through a number of additional cable cars. Among the steepest and most thrilling is the cable car at Fajã dos Padres!

Take a hike on a levada. Numerous levadas—tiny water channels—that were constructed throughout the island have been transformed into hiking routes. Two of the most well-liked hikes are the Caldeirão Verde and the 25 Fountains levada hikes.

Check out the gardens. In addition to providing fantastic views of the city below, the botanical gardens and the Asian-style gardens of Monte Palace in Funchal are definitely worth a visit.

Take a road excursion. The greatest way to see Madeira is by vehicle. The north of Madeira is an absolute blast to drive through, especially the stretch between Sao Vicente and Porto da Cruz. The west side of the island is also a terrific place to go on a road trip if you enjoy winding mountain roads and breathtaking coastal views.

Swim in the natural pools and beaches. Given the scarcity of beaches, Madeira isn't really an island for "beach vacations". There are, however, a number of man-made sandy beaches, numerous pebble beaches, and a number of naturally occurring saltwater pools, most notably near Porto Moniz.

Look around the mountains. Madeira's inner regions in the center provide some of the most breathtaking views. It's imperative to hike to Pico Ruivo! You can also take the Nuns Valley trek or travel to the town of Curral das Freiras, where you can take in the beautiful mountain views.

Take a boat ride. Going out to sea is especially worthwhile if you want to have a possibility of seeing whales or dolphins. During the months of May through September, when whales and dolphins are most common, several whale-watching trips leave from Madeira.

9. Remember to pack.

Just pack for the vacation as you normally would. If you want to go trekking, don't forget to pack comfy shoes. Even in the summer, pack a sweater and raincoat in addition to your beachwear and flip-flops (just in case, especially for higher elevations).

10. Pick up a few Portuguese words.

Even if the majority of the population speaks English, it's still beneficial to pick up some local vernacular.

Most significantly, the pronunciation of Madeira differs from that of "deer". The pronunciation in Portuguese is more akin to "mad - aye - ra". Locals will be more impressed if you say it in Portuguese, but they will still understand if you say "ma - deer - ah".

Other terms to become familiar with:

Hi - hola!

Boa Tarde, Boa Noite, Dom Dia - Good Morning, Afternoon, and Night

Expressing gratitude with a obrigado (for men) or obrigada (for women)

Per favor, please.

Thank you very much - De nada

Remember that you're not in Spain, and the Portuguese are a little miffed at being misinterpreted as Spanish! Although there are some parallels between Spanish and Portuguese, English is usually the recommended foreign language to learn first.

The Portuguese dialect spoken on Madeira differs significantly from that of the Portuguese mainland, often making comprehension more difficult for native speakers. Some of the thicker-accented Madeiran Portuguese may be more difficult to follow if you already know some Brazilian or continental Portuguese. Never hesitate to use English; you won't offend anyone if you do.

Madeira is it safe? (Advice for a secure visit)

Madeira has a relatively low crime rate, making it a highly safe place to visit. But in addition to criminality, there are other crucial safety factors that you should be aware of.

First of all, if you're not used to driving on the right or are an unskilled driver, driving on the island can be difficult. You will undoubtedly encounter numerous curves and turns because Madeira is extremely mountainous, especially when you leave the main highways.

However, the mountains can still be dangerous if you refuse to drive. There have been a few disastrous incidents where hikers have fallen from high cliffs or even when they have taken too many steps back while posing for photos.

In general, Madeira is safe, although regrettably, it happens frequently that misbehavior by tourists causes accidents that make the local headlines. If you're careless, Madeira could be dangerous.

Safety and crime

Portugal is generally a very safe country, but the small island of Madeira is much safer. There is really little cause for concern when it comes to personal safety in Madeira because violent crimes involving tourists are incredibly infrequent.

However, it's crucial to follow standard travel safety procedures when visiting any place, including hiding or keeping your valuables close to hand, especially at night. Though uncommon, pickpocketing is always a possibility, especially in Funchal.

Are there certain places to stay away from?

There are no particular regions that tourists should stay away from because of crime. Even if there aren't many "bad areas," it's a good idea to exercise cautious and keep a watch on any valuables.

Safe hiking

Thanks in part to its relatively difficult pathways with mountain cliffs, waterfalls, and plenty of levadas (irrigation systems), hiking is a very popular pastime in Madeira. Boat rides and other water sports are among the many outdoor activities made possible by the island's distinct climate.

To be honest, these outdoor activities pose the greatest threats to one's safety in Madeira.

Even though hiking routes are often well-kept and safe, there have occasionally been tales of people disappearing or experiencing worse.

For instance, a hiker on the Levada das 25 Fontes passed away in 2023. Although there is typically minimal risk associated with this trip, accidents serve as a warning that careless behavior can still result in harm or worse. A tourist lost his life in 2023 while posing for pictures at the well-known Cascata dos Anjos waterfall. Before falling thirty meters, it appears that the individual may have stood on the stone road barricades along the edge.

Not to sound alarmist, but it's important to exercise caution!

Advice on how to be safe when trekking

For information on potential hazards and difficulty levels, consult the official trail descriptions. Sometimes trails are closed due to natural disasters like mudslides. You can also obtain the official booklet on this government website, which includes estimated times and other information, by clicking the info icons adjacent to the trails.

Be mindful of any potential dangers, such as loose pebbles or slick surfaces, when trekking along levadas. Follow only the official trails (many unmarked levadas aren't meant to be walked; pay attention to any signs prohibiting you from doing so).

Avoid taking risks or taking pictures from precipices in order to capture the "ultimate selfie," as you can find yourself in a Darwin Award scenario.

The weather might change suddenly. Make sure you bring the right items and keep an eye on the forecast.

The well-known Pico de Areiro to Pico Ruivo walk contains some extremely narrow stairs on the edge of a mountain rim, so proceed with caution. There are sections where the only thing keeping you from plummeting down a precipice is a single horizontal rope. While it's still fairly doable for any reasonable adult, some tourists have asked if they can accomplish this while carrying a baby, which is absolutely not a good idea!

Swimming and beaches safety

While Madeira isn't exactly known for being a beach vacation spot, the island does have a number of beaches where you may enjoy some water sports.

Lifeguards watch over certain beaches in Madeira. Machico Beach is among the beaches with the best security. This artificial beach is especially great for families and has golden sand.

There are natural pools in various parts of Madeira, such Porto Moniz, for a distinctive swimming experience. These lava-rock-formed pools offer a safe haven where you may swim in shallow water without worrying about the waves.

However, surfers and adventurers are also drawn to Madeira's sea waves; they frequently choose spots like Praia da Prainha and Seixal Beach.

The swimming safety conditions are indicated by the flag system. A green flag indicates that swimming is safe in the water, but a yellow flag warns of potential severe currents or waves. Lastly, a red sign indicates that swimming is not advised because of dangerous conditions.

Is driving in Madeira safe?

Since local, experienced drivers are accustomed to handling Madeira's roadways, taking a taxi, bus, or private tour service is probably the safest option for getting around.

If you want to hire a car in Madeira and go about the island on your own, you should be aware that the island's tiny, twisting roads and steep inclines can make driving difficult at times.

To be very honest, after reading so many cautions online, we had much lower expectations for our first-ever trip to Madeira. Actually, the majority of Madeira's main thoroughfares—including the expressways and the direct routes that pass through lengthy, straight tunnels—are quite simple to drive.

Still, it's true that the ancient ER101 coastal roads and side roads can be a little more daring. For this reason, having some prior experience driving in the mountains may be beneficial. Your opinions about driving will undoubtedly vary depending on your own driving history, how much you drive on smaller mountain roads, and whether you're used to driving on the right.

Going to Madeira alone

Is it possible to go alone in Madeira? Of course! The island is a great option for anyone going on a solo journey because of its reputation for safety and friendliness.

It's also very acceptable for a female traveler to go alone to Madeira. Madeira has been rated favorably by many women as a suitable destination for solitary female travel.

When traveling alone, getting about will definitely be your biggest issue because there isn't a lot of public transit. You could choose to rent a car, but public transportation is also an option if you don't mind having slightly less options.

If you choose to hike alone, exercise caution; it's usually preferable to choose a well-traveled trail or go with a group. To participate in an activity with others, you might choose to schedule tours (such as guided hikes or boat trips).

Madeira has a number of excellent hostels for lone travelers. The island wasn't previously well-known as a backpacking or hosteling destination, but in recent years, that has all changed, with a number of inexpensive hostels popping up, mostly in Funchal.

Packing Necessities

Avoid Bringing a Portable Speaker

First things first: you might want to think twice before carrying that portable speaker if you're planning a trip to one of Portugal's beaches. Portugal took a firm stand in 2023 to preserve the peaceful environment along its coastline.

A rule prohibiting the use of portable speakers to play loud music on beaches was passed by the National Maritime Authority. And they mean business, I assure you. The sanctions may be as much as €36,000 or as little as €200. For that reason, if you are going to pack your JBL speaker for a beach day, remember to leave it at home.

1 Pack Thin Layers

Alright, allow me to share a small secret with you: Madeira boasts the trendiest climate on the planet!

It's true that you can be scorching hot on the beach one moment and freezing your ass off in the mountains thirty minutes later!

This isn't limited to altitude either—traveling from one island shore to the next can expose you to an entirely different ecology in a matter of minutes! Imagine going from hot and dry to overcast, windy, and wet!

It's strange, yes, but that's Madeira for ya!

For this reason, when it comes to packing for your trip here, layers are always a wise choice.

My top recommendation for your Madeira checklist is to wear lightweight clothing that you can remove or wear as the weather changes. This is the greatest approach to be prepared for every situation, no matter what kind of weather you face.

This is particularly true if you're coming here in the spring or fall, in which case layering your clothing to make sure you're covering all bases and avoid overpacking is essential!

2 Don't Get Heavy!

Speaking of light, it's worth spending a little time discussing how to pack everything you need for Madeira without bringing too much with you!

Considering that most visitors to Madeira will be bringing hiking boots, we all know all too well how hefty these things can be!

However, if you wear your hiking boots to the airport and pack wisely (which this list will help you do), you should be able to fit all you'll need for this island stay into a medium-sized carry-on luggage or a 40–50l backpack.

You have no justification because I never bring anything larger, even when I travel for two to six months at a time!

Osprey's 50l Aura backpack is a fantastic option for a backpack, and it would look amazing when paired with some excellent packing cubes!

Packing cubes, my friends, are the solution to all of your luggage issues! If you want to compact your belongings and keep them neatly organized, I strongly advise getting some!

I adore these Osprey packing cubes and would never, ever consider traveling to Madeira—or anyplace else, for that matter—without them!

3 Hiking Gear Packing

Additionally, even though this packing list is meant to be as light as possible, it still includes everything you'll need to enjoy some of the greatest vacation experiences in Madeira.

First up, hiking is the main reason most people—including myself—come to this island in the first place.

Being a coastal nation with a mountain range in the middle, Madeira experiences frequent strong winds. For this reason, a thin, light, waterproof, and windproof jacket will be quite helpful to have!

Since some of the mountain trails in Madeira are rather steep, I also advise hiking boots over walking shoes. You'll definitely appreciate the added traction and ankle support that boots provide.

When hiking, don't forget to bring a sturdy day pack to accommodate all of your belongings. This will assist your shoulders bear the weight more equally.

I also never go hiking without a power pack. This guarantees that I can always charge my phone, and Anker is my preferred brand in this regard.

I actually own two of their power packs; one is charged in my lodging and is carried with me during the day. These are ready to be switched out.

I often bring an extra battery for my large camera with me on hikes so I can switch it out and continuing taking pictures wherever I go!

Lastly, I suggest wearing clothing with lots of pockets for trekking so you can quickly access items like water, food, hand sanitizer, tissues, and cameras.

4 Beach Gear Packing

Without a doubt, packing a beach towel and some swimsuit is a smart idea for Madeira.

On this island, the majority of the beaches are stony or have black sand; however, there are a few with white sand at Machico and Calheta. Whichever kind of shoreline you choose, you simply must go for a swim and lay in the sun to dry off!

A sunscreen with at least 30 SPF and UV-protected sunglasses are also excellent additions to your Madeira packing list, particularly during the summer when temperatures can soar.

In addition, I would suggest packing a decent moisturizer for Madeira that you can apply on your hands, body, and face after spending the day in the sun. Lastly, don't forget to pack a dry bag and a handy sarong to keep your belongings safe and sand-free on the beach (particularly any electronics).

A rash vest and a wetsuit can be useful additions if you also intend to surf in Madeira.

5. Got Ready for Funchal

Since Madeira is a liberal western European island, you can definitely go about in shorts and a t-shirt when you're in the capital city of Funchal or any other town in the region.

But keep in mind that the weather might vary, and that spring and fall bring with them cooler evenings. Don't forget to bring at least one pair of pants and a few lightweight sweaters.

Since most restaurants in Madeira are extremely casual and you typically don't need to wear formal attire while dining out, these will also be ideal for eating in.

One thing you should be prepared for while visiting Madeira is that it appears like every town and village is situated on a steep slope (!). This means that exploring the area will require you to trek up hills a lot, which will strain your calves!

For this reason, I strongly advise bringing supportive sandals like Arizona Birkenstocks or lightweight sneakers for Madeira.

Lastly, if you want to stay hydrated while traveling, it's a good idea to bring a metal water bottle, such as this Kleen Kanteen, as the tap water on this island is safe to drink.

Entire Madeira Packing List

Here is my comprehensive packing list for Madeira, which includes a detailed item-by-item description of everything you need to bring!

The quantity of each item you need depends depend on how long you plan to remain on the island, but as a starting point, here is a list of everything you should bring.

Again, if you pack carefully, you should be able to fit everything into a medium backpack or compact suitcase, which is ideal for storing items overhead on flights and preventing baggage costs!

CLOTHES

Waterproof, Windproof, Lightweight Jacket

Active fleece, sweater, or thin sweater

T-shirts and singlets

Either jeans or evening pants

Casual Day Trousers for Hiking

Trousers

Cutoffs

Dresses casual or jumpsuits

Undies and Socks

Swimsuits

Wraps, Buffs, and Scarves

Clothing for the night

FITNESS

Sneakers

Shoes / Pumps

Athletic Boots

UTILITIES

Minimal Toiletry Pouch with Hook

Bars of Shampoo and Conditioner

Bactericidal Soap

Defecation

Toner, Moisturizer, Serum, and Face Cleanser

Body Lotion / Post-Sun

Sunscreen SPF

SPF Moisturizer

Toothpaste, toothbrush, and floss

Shaver with Extra Blades

Nail File and Scissors

Tiny Tongs

Pads / Buds of Cotton

Hair Clips

Electronics

Bluetooth headphones and smartphones

Carry-Along Battery

Good GoPro and camera

Chargers, Memory Card, Lens, and Extra Battery

European Plug

Headlight and Extra Batteries

OTHER MATTER!

Contact lenses or glasses, if you wear them

UV-protective sunglasses

Earplugs with an eye mask

Daily Sack

A dry bag

Bottle of Water

Beach towel and sarong

Trip Protection

ID card and driver's license

A bank card such as Wise can help you receive better exchange rates and save money on foreign transaction fees.

Cash in Euros

Things to pack for your safety and well-being.

Some of these items might not apply to you and your travel itinerary, and you might not be able to buy and bring them all. Discuss with your physician the things that are most crucial to you.

Since it's a generic list, it might not contain all you need.

In the event that your trip is delayed, don't forget to bring additional essential medical supplies.

Prescription drugs

Your medication

Medication for diarrhea in tourists

Syringe and suture kit

Your doctor must write a letter on letterhead stationery for the kit to be used by your local healthcare practitioner.

Medicine for altitude sickness

Medical equipment

Eyewear

Think about bringing extra glasses in case yours are broken.

Contact lenses.

If you think your contacts might be broken, think about taking extras.

Syringes or needles (for example, for diabetes)

Needs a letter on letterhead stationery from your physician

Surgical kit

Your doctor must write a letter on letterhead stationery for the kit to be used by your local healthcare practitioner.

Supplies for testing for diabetes

Insulin.

Halters

Auto-injectors of epinephrine (EpiPens)

A necklace or bracelet with medical alerts

Nonprescription medications

Medication for diarrhea

Examples include bismuth subsalicylate (Pepto-Bismol) and loperamide (Imodium).

Antidiabetic

Medication for motion sickness

Drops of cough

Suppressant/expectorant for cough

Reducing agent

Medication for heat and pain

Acetaminophen, aspirin, or ibuprofen are a few examples.

A light laxative

Some kind of sleep aid or mild sedative

Salted nasal mist

Supplies to shield against disease or damage

Wipes or hand sanitizers

Antibacterial hand wipes or alcohol-based hand sanitizer with at least 60% alcohol

Tablets for water purification

Refer to the CDC's advice on water disinfection.

Repetant to insects

According to the CDC's advice, use an insect repellent to prevent bug bites.

Melathrin

Permethrin is a clothes insect repellent. If you spend a lot of time outside, it can be necessary. Clothes can also be pre-treated at home.

Sunblock

(SPF 15 or higher) that offers both UVB and UVA defense. See Exposure to Sun.

A hat and shades

Put on to get more protection from the sun. The perfect hat has a wide brim.

Individual safety gear

Bicycle helmets and child safety seats are two examples.

Tinnituses

Rubber condoms

First-aid supply

1% cream hydrocortisone

The antifungal creams

Antimicrobial creams

Antiseptic cleaner for wounds

Gel aloe

For tanlines

Management of insect bites

Anti-itch cream or gel

scabs

Adhesive tape, gauze, and multiple sizes

For blisters, use moleskin or molefoam.

Compression/elastic bandage wrap

For aches and bruises

Single-use gloves

Thermometer digital

Safety pins and scissors

Swabs of cotton (Q-Tips)

Tiny Tongs

Eyelid swabs

Salts for oral rehydration

Records

Documentation for health insurance

Copies of claim forms and your health insurance card (from your primary plan or any additional travel health insurance plan)

All prescription copies

Verify if generic names are included with prescriptions. Bring prescription medications, contact lenses or eyeglasses, and additional medical supplies.

Visiting card

Keep a contact card with the following people's street addresses, phone numbers, and email addresses on it:

A close relative or acquaintance who is still in the United States

Home health care provider or providers

Accommodations when you get there

Hospitals or clinics in your destination that offer emergency services

US consulate or embassy in the country or countries of destination

Recommended itineraries for Madeira
MADEIRA TWO-DAY PROGRAMME

Day 1.

Morning walk along the coast at Ponta de São Lourenço

Early afternoon: See the houses and have lunch in Santana.

Late afternoon stroll along Pico Ruivo

Evening: Funchal dinner

Day Two

Morning: Viewpoints of Pico do Arieiro

Late morning: Skywalk at Cabo Girão

Cascata Dos Anjos and lunch by the coast in the early afternoon

At midday, Porto Moniz

Fanal forest in the late afternoon

3-Day Itinerary for Madeira

Follow the instructions for Days 1 and 2 of this 3-day itinerary in Madeira, and then on Day 3...

Morning: Monte Palace Tropical Gardens and the Funchal cable car

Late in the day: A toboggan trip

Early afternoon: Take a stroll around Funchal's streets and eat lunch at any fine restaurant.

After midafternoon: Unwind a little. If your hotel doesn't have a pool, visit Praia Formosa or one of the lidos by the waterfront.

4-Day Itinerary for Madeira

If you extend your stay, you'll have more time to enjoy some longer hikes without having to skip other sites. Alternatively, you might schedule additional downtime—after all, you are on vacation!

Day 1

Investigate the island's eastern flank. For example, Santana, the Cabo Girão Skywalk, Ponta de São Lourenço, and Caniço

Next, Day 2

Take the day to tour the island's western region. The Cascata Dos Anjos Waterfall, the west coast viewpoints, the Achadas da Cruz cable car, Porto Moniz, and Fanal are all visible when traveling clockwise from Funchal.

Day 3 follows.

It's time for a long walk today. One well-liked route is Pico do Arieiro to Pico Ruivo. Furthermore, a transportation company can be hired to drop you off at one location and pick you up at another. If not, there are numerous options for Levado walks.

And lastly, Day Four

If the weather is nice, spend the morning touring Funchal, including the Tropical Gardens and the cable car. Then, make sure to unwind for a while. In addition, you'll undoubtedly have sore legs from yesterday's long stroll!

A five-day schedule providing an overview of the main island

Day 1: Funchal - Take a cable car ride and take in the atmosphere of the largest city in Madeira;

Day 2: Porto Moniz: Take a dip in the most beautiful natural pools on the main island of Madeira;

Day 3: Levada of Caldeirão Verde - After hiking one of Madeira's most well-known routes, take lots of Instagram-worthy photos;

Day 4: Santana - Visit one of Madeira's friendliest towns and take in the renowned Santana homes;

Day 5: Caniçal and return to Funchal - Take part in some diving, have some dinner at the Aquarium or Muralhas restaurants, and then return to the airport.

7-day schedule: seeing Desertas/Selvagens and the main island

Day 1: Funchal - Take a cable car trip and take in the atmosphere of the largest city in Madeira.

Day 2: Porto Moniz: Take a dip in the most beautiful natural pools on the main island of Madeira;

Day 3: Levada of Caldeirão Verde - After hiking one of Madeira's most well-known routes, take lots of Instagram-worthy photos;

Day 4: Desertas and/or Selvagens - Have a close-up look at the little, deserted archipelagos of Desertas and Selvagens by taking one of two boat cruises;

Day 5: Fanal and Cape Girão - Witness Madeira's breathtaking scenery from two of the island's top vantage points;

Day 6: Santana - Visit one of Madeira's friendliest towns and take in the renowned Santana homes;

Day 7: Caniçal and return to Funchal - Take part in some diving, have some dinner at the Aquarium or Muralhas restaurants, and then return to the airport.

10-day schedule: A comprehensive exploration of Madeira

Day 1: Funchal - Take a cable car ride and take in the atmosphere of the largest city in Madeira;

Day 2: Porto Moniz: Take a dip in the most beautiful natural pools on the main island of Madeira;

Day 3: Levada of Caldeirão Verde - After hiking one of Madeira's most well-known routes, take lots of Instagram-worthy photos;

Day 4: Fanal and Cape Girão - Witness Madeira's breathtaking scenery from two of the island's top vantage points;

Days 5-7: Porto Santo - Enjoy the beautiful white sand beaches of Porto Santo by taking your time and unwinding;

Day 8: Desertas and/or Selvagens - Witness up close the small, deserted archipelagos of Desertas and Selvagens by taking one or two boat cruises;

Day 9: Santana - Visit one of Madeira's friendliest communities and take in the renowned Santana homes;

Day 10: Caniçal and return to Funchal - Take part in some diving, have some dinner at the Aquarium or Muralhas restaurants, and then return to the airport.

CONCLUSION

As we approach the last part of our exploration of the alluring world of Madeira, I feel forced to share a profound truth: this magical island is not just a place to visit; it is an experience that will change you from the inside out. Your journey has just begun for those who have been itching to discover the mysteries of this emerald treasure in the broad Atlantic.

We have walked across craggy peaks that reach the sky and seen the boundless expanse of the ocean on our journey. We've traveled far into old woodlands where towering trees and placid Levadas coexist with the echoes of long before. We have danced to the beat of vivid festivals and music in Madeira, and we have enjoyed delectable cuisine that transcends countries and traditions.

But allow me to highlight a few things that you shouldn't miss on your first trip to Madeira, dear reader:

Pico do Arieiro: Take in the breathtaking view and crisp air of Madeira's highest point. You will never forget the moment you touched the sky and felt the entire planet beneath your feet.

Laurissilva Forest: Let the whispers of nature's wisdom envelop your soul as you immerse yourself in the heart of an old woodland. The Laurissilva is a haven for those who find comfort in its embrace and a living example of the beauty that endures over time.

Mercado dos Lavradores: Enter a lively marketplace filled with a convergence of scents and vivid hues. Savour unique fruits, take in the artistry of handcrafted items, and allow the warmth of Madeira's culture to embrace you as if it were the embrace of a long-lost friend.

Fado Music: Allow the eerie melodies of Fado music to take you to a different era and location where the most profound feelings of the soul are expressed. The musical legacy of the island serves as a link to its history and a request to participate in its tales.

Levada Walks: Follow the mild streams that meander through the center of the island to discover undiscovered waterfalls, verdant surroundings, and the peace of a more laid-back, slower way of life. Your path to tranquility is this.

Finally, I would like to extend an invitation to you, my dear reader, to continue on this incredible voyage by seeing Madeira for yourself. It is a place that calls to the inquisitive, the daring, and the admirer of beauty. It is a place where transformations are promised in addition to memories.

Madeira's verdant surroundings, lively culture, and kind locals will welcome you with open arms. Get ready to be captivated by a location where daily encounters with nature's marvels occur, where awe-inspiring sunsets color the sky, and where every step takes you closer to the center of adventure.

The time has come to set out on your own Madeira odyssey. Let the enchantment of the island enchant you; cast aside your fears and embrace the unknown. It is an invitation to experience life to the fullest, to enjoy the wonders of the globe, and to make treasured memories that will permanently brighten the fabric of your existence rather than merely a destination.

Take a tour of Madeira right away, and allow the ageless charm of this island to enchant you forever.

dc8b8724-a7b0-484f-805b-2d55c4a25aabR02